CONTENTS

About The "Words & Wisdom" Series

Inspired by the works of his great-great grandfather Edward S. Ellis, R. Scott Frothingham has published the "Words & Wisdom" series featuring American historical figures -- including Abraham Lincoln, Benjamin Franklin, Theodore Roosevelt, Mark Twain and others. Frothingham explains:

> Growing up, I loved the living room in my grandmother's house in Rye, NY. The room featured a fireplace, a grand piano and two floor-to-ceiling built-in bookshelves taking up the entire walls on either side of a French door to the 3-season screened porch.

> Those shelves were entirely filled with books written by her grandfather "Grampy Ellis". A good number of those books were read aloud to me, and as I grew older, I read many to myself; always amazed that one of my relatives had been such a prolific author and delighting in the exploits of Deerfoot and other tales of frontier adventure.

> One of the first books I read from Ellis' later life -- when he had shifted from dime novels to more serious work -- was *Thomas Jefferson -A Character Sketch*. Fondly remembering the discovery of that book, I thought I would celebrate Edward S. Ellis's love of America, history and biographies by giving readers a slightly different look at some important Americans and the events surrounding their lives, by letting those historical figures speak for themselves.

Thus, the "Words & Wisdom" series was conceived -- featuring selections of the actual words of historical figures -- to offer a better understanding of the people behind the beloved icons and notable events we are presented in brief during grade school.

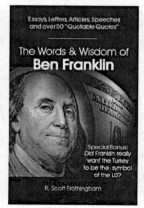

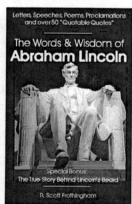

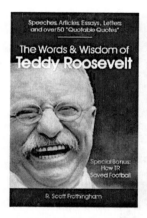

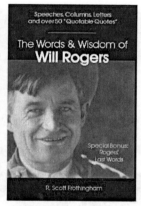

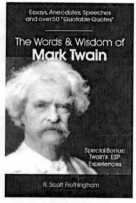

"The Words & Wisdom of Teddy Roosevelt" is dedicated to
Edward S. Ellis' great-great-great granddaughter
Katharine Mason Frothingham

As a **"Thank You"** for purchasing this book, here is a **FREE** eBook:
"Thomas Jefferson – A Character Sketch" – get your copy at:
www.EdwardSEllis.com/Thank-You-(TJ).html

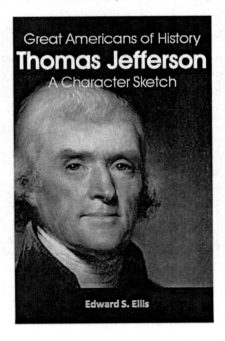

Publisher's Preface

Theodore Roosevelt, the 26th President of the United States, is a beloved figure in American history and is perhaps the most quoted of all the presidents (along with his fellow honorees on Mount Rushmore: George Washington, Thomas Jefferson and Abraham Lincoln).

You might be familiar with his famous:

> *It is not the critic who counts; not the man who points out how the strong man stumbles, or where the doer of deeds could have done them better. The credit belongs to the man who is actually in the arena, whose face is marred by dust and sweat and blood; who strives valiantly; who errs, and comes short again and again, because there is no effort without error and shortcoming; but who does actually strive to do the deeds; who knows the great enthusiasms, the great devotions; who spends himself in a worthy cause; who at the best knows in the end the triumph of high achievement, and who at the worst, if he fails, at least fails while daring greatly, so that his place shall never be with those cold and timid souls who know neither victory nor defeat.*

What was the context for that quote? When was it delivered? Why? As a fan of that quote and Teddy Roosevelt, you'll be interested to learn that it was part of a speech delivered in in Paris on April 23, 1910: "Citizenship in a Republic." On page 56 you can read the entire text of that speech.

Also included is a copy of "The Leader and the Cause" speech (known as "It Takes More Than That to Kill a Bull Moose"). On October 14, 1912, on his way to make a speech in Milwaukee, Roosevelt was shot in an assassination attempt by John Schrank. Undeterred, TR started his address with:

> *Friends, I shall ask you to be as quiet as possible. I don't know whether you fully understand that I have just been shot; but it takes more than that to kill a Bull Moose. But fortunately I had my manuscript, so you see I was going to make a long speech, and there is a bullet—there is where the bullet went through—and it probably saved me from it going into my heart. The bullet is in me now, so that I cannot make a very long speech, but I will try my best.*

Inside you will also find a portion of Roosevelt's 1893 book, "The Wilderness Hunter", in which he shares a tale about Bigfoot/Sasquatch and 3 articles that sum up TR's approach to life: "Character and Success", "The American Boy" and "The Strenuous Life".

There is also a letter that lead up to a most controversial dinner and personal diary entries about a heartbreakingly emotional serries of events.

I hope you find all of these words interesting (and at times inspirational and motivational) and that they help you gain a deeper and more personal understanding of Teddy Roosevelt, one of the great characters in history.

R. Scott Frothingham
Vienna, VA

NOTE: As we are using the actual words of Theodore Roosevelt, throughout this book you will find examples of spelling, word choice and grammar that differ from today's standards, we have purposely not changed or updated the original text.

Quotable Quotes from TR

Before we get to the long-form pieces, let's take a look at some of the great "sound bite" quotes attributed to this "larger-than-life" figure from the past.

If you could kick the person in the pants responsible for most of your trouble, you wouldn't sit for a month.

I am only an average man but, by George, I work harder at it than the average man.

It is hard to fail, but it is worse never to have tried to succeed.

Keep your eyes on the stars, and your feet on the ground.

A man who has never gone to school may steal from a freight car; but if he has a university education, he may steal the whole railroad.

It is difficult to make our material condition better by the best law, but it is easy enough to ruin it by bad laws.

With self-discipline most anything is possible.

In any moment of decision, the best thing you can do is the right thing, the next best thing is the wrong thing, and the worst thing you can do is nothing.

Big jobs usually go to the men who prove their ability to outgrow small ones.

The best executive is one who has sense enough to pick good people to do what he wants done, and self-restraint enough to keep from meddling with them while they do it.

Great thoughts speak only to the thoughtful mind, but great actions speak to all mankind.

I took the Canal Zone and let Congress debate; and while the debate goes on, the canal does also.

I care not what others think of what I do, but I care very much about what I think of what I do! That is character!

It behooves every man to remember that the work of the critic is of altogether secondary importance, and that, in the end, progress is accomplished by the man who does things.

Knowing what's right doesn't mean much unless you do what's right.

I don't pity any man who does hard work worth doing. I admire him. I pity the creature who does not work, at whichever end of the social scale he may regard himself as being.

Do what you can, with what you have, where you are.

Get action. Seize the moment. Man was never intended to become an oyster.

I think there is only one quality worse than hardness of heart and that is softness of head.

I am a part of everything that I have read.

If there is not the war, you don't get the great general; if there is not a great occasion, you don't get a great statesman; if Lincoln had lived in a time of peace, no one would have known his name.

Character, in the long run, is the decisive factor in the life of an individual and of nations alike.

Believe you can and you're halfway there.

It is only through labor and painful effort, by grim energy and resolute courage, that we move on to better things.

A man who is good enough to shed his blood for the country is good enough to be given a square deal afterwards.

When you are asked if you can do a job, tell 'em, 'Certainly I can!' Then get busy and find out how to do it.

Appraisals are where you get together with your team leader and agree what an outstanding member of the team you are, how much your contribution has been valued, what massive potential you have and, in recognition of all this, would you mind having your salary halved.

Behind the ostensible government sits enthroned an invisible government owing no allegiance and acknowledging no responsibility to the people.

Courtesy is as much a mark of a gentleman as courage.

Don't hit at all if it is honorably possible to avoid hitting; but never hit soft.

A typical vice of American politics is the avoidance of saying anything real on real issues.

Courage is not having the strength to go on; it is going on when you don't have the strength.".

Far and away the best prize that life has to offer is the chance to work hard at work worth doing.

The human body has two ends on it: one to create with and one to sit on. Sometimes people get their ends reversed. When this happens they need a kick in the seat of the pants.

To announce that there must be no criticism of the President, or that we are to stand by the President, right or wrong, is not only unpatriotic and servile, but is morally treasonable to the American public.

Far better is it to dare mighty things, to win glorious triumphs, even though checkered by failure... than to rank with those poor spirits who neither enjoy nor suffer much, because they live in a gray twilight that knows not victory nor defeat.

No man is worth his salt who is not ready at all times to risk his well-being, to risk his body, to risk his life, in a great cause.

For unflagging interest and enjoyment, a household of children, if things go reasonably well, certainly all other forms of success and achievement lose their importance by comparison.

Never throughout history has a man who lived a life of ease left a name worth remembering.

Nine-tenths of wisdom is being wise in time.

No man is justified in doing evil on the ground of expedience.

Old age is like everything else

Some men can live up to their loftiest ideals without ever going higher than a basement.

Nobody cares how much you know, until they know how much you care.

To make a success of it, you've got to start young. Every reform movement has a lunatic fringe.

When you play, play hard; when you work, don't play at all.

Order without liberty and liberty without order are equally destructive.

People ask the difference between a leader and a boss. The leader leads, and the boss drives.

The first requisite of a good citizen in this republic of ours is that he shall be able and willing to pull his own weight.

Rhetoric is a poor substitute for action, and we have trusted only to rhetoric. If we are really to be a great nation, we must not merely talk; we must act big.

The boy who is going to make a great man must not make up his mind merely to overcome a thousand obstacles, but to win in spite of a thousand repulses and defeats.

The most important single ingredient in the formula of success is knowing how to get along with people.

The one thing I want to leave my children is an honorable name.

The only man who never makes a mistake is the man who never does anything.

Freedom from effort in the present merely means that there has been effort stored up in the past.

and, finally, perhaps his most remembered and repeated:

Speak softly and carry a big stick; you will go far.

About that famous quote: During Roosevelt's term as Governor of NY State he battled with the party bosses regarding a political appointment. And, although Boss Tom Platt threatened to "ruin" him, Roosevelt held out and eventually got his way.

According to "Theodore Roosevelt, A Life" by Nathan Miller (pg 337):

"Looking back upon his handling of the incident, Roosevelt thought he 'never saw a bluff carried more resolutely through to the final limit.' And writing to a friend a few days later, he observed: 'I have always been fond of the West African proverb: *"Speak softly and carry a big stick; you will go far."* ' "

Teddy and Bigfoot

In Roosevelt's 1893 book, *The Wilderness Hunter*, he shares a tale told by Bauman, a German trapper who was trapping with a friend near the Salmon River in the Bitterroot Mountains (somewhere between Idaho and Montana). Did they encounter Bigfoot?

Frontiersmen are not, as a rule, apt to be very superstitious. They lead lives too hard and practical, and have too little imagination in things spiritual and supernatural.

I have heard but few ghost stories while living on the frontier, and those few were of a perfectly commonplace and conventional type. But I once listened to a goblin-story, which rather impressed me.

It was told by a grizzled, weather beaten old mountain hunter, named Bauman who, born and had passed all of his life on the Frontier, told it the story to me. He must have believed what he said, for he could hardly repress a shudder at certain points of the tale; but he was of German ancestry, and in childhood had doubtless been saturated with all kinds of ghost and goblin lore. So that many fearsome superstitions were latent in his mind; besides, he knew well the stories told by the Indian medicine men in their winter camps, of the snow-walkers, and the specters, [spirits, ghosts & apparitions] the formless evil beings that haunt the forest depths, and dog and waylay the lonely wanderer who after nightfall passes through the regions where they lurk. It may be that when overcome by the horror of the fate that befell his friend, and when oppressed by the awful dread of the unknown, he grew to attribute, both at the time and still more in remembrance, weird and elfin traits to what was merely some abnormally wicked and cunning wild beast; but whether this was so or not, no man can say.

When the event occurred, Bauman was still a young man, and was trapping with a partner among the mountains dividing the forks of the Salmon from the head of Wisdom River. Not having had much luck, he and his partner determined to go up into a particularly wild and lonely pass through which ran a small stream said to contain many beaver.

The pass had an evil reputation because the year before a solitary hunter who had wandered into it was slain, seemingly by a wild beast, the half eaten remains being afterwards found by some mining prospectors who had passed his camp only the night before.

The memory of this event, however, weighted very lightly with the two trappers, who were as adventurous and hardy as others of their kind. They took their two lean mountain ponies to the foot of the pass where they left them in an open beaver meadow, the rocky timber-clad ground being from there onward impracticable for horses.

They then struck out on foot through the vast, gloomy forest, and in about four hours reached a little open glade where they concluded to camp, as signs of game were plenty.

There was still an hour or two of daylight left, and after building a brush lean-to and throwing down and opening their packs, they started upstream. The country was very dense and hard to travel through, as there was much down timber, although here and there the somber woodland was broken by small glades of mountain grass. At dusk they again reached camp. The glade in which it was pitched was not many yards wide, the tall, close-set pines and firs rising round it like a wall. On one side was a little stream, beyond which rose the steep mountains slope, covered with the unbroken growth of evergreen forest.

They were surprised to find that during their absence something, apparently a bear, had visited camp, and had rummaged about among their things, scattering the contents of their packs, and in sheer wantonness destroying their lean-to. The footprints of the beast were quite plain, but at first they paid no particular heed to them, busying themselves with rebuilding the lean-to, laying out their beds and stores and lighting the fire.

While Bauman was making ready supper, it being already dark, his companion began to examine the tracks more closely, and soon took a brand from the fire to follow them up, where the intruder had walked along a game trail after leaving the camp. When the brand flickered out, he returned and took another, repeating his inspection of the footprints very closely. Coming back to the fire, he stood by it a minute or two, peering out into the darkness, and suddenly remarked, "Bauman, that bear has been walking on two legs."

Bauman laughed at this, but his partner insisted that he was right, and upon again examining the tracks with a torch, they certainly did seem to be made by but two paws or feet. However, it was too dark to make sure. After discussing whether the footprints could possibly be those of a human being, and coming to the conclusion that they could not be, the two men rolled up in their blankets, and went to sleep under the lean-to. At midnight Bauman was awakened by some noise, and sat up in his blankets. As he did so his nostrils were struck by a strong, wild-beast odor, and he caught the loom of a great body in the darkness at the mouth of the lean-to. Grasping his rifle, he fired at the vague, threatening shadow, but must have missed, for immediately afterwards he heard the smashing of the under wood as the thing, whatever it was, rushed off into the impenetrable blackness of the forest and the night.

After this the two men slept but little, sitting up by the rekindled fire, but they heard nothing more. In the morning they started out to look at the few traps they had set the previous evening and put out new ones. By an unspoken agreement they kept together all day, and returned to camp towards evening. On nearing it they saw, hardly to their astonishment that the lean-to had again been torn down. The visitor of the preceding day had returned, and in wanton malice had tossed about their camp kit and bedding, and destroyed the shanty. The ground was marked up by its tracks, and on leaving the camp it had gone along the soft earth by the brook. The footprints were as plain as if on snow, and, after a careful scrutiny of the trail, it certainly did seem as if, whatever the thing was, it had walked off on but two legs.

The men, thoroughly uneasy, gathered a great heap of dead logs and kept up a roaring fire throughout the night, one or the other sitting on guard most of the time. About midnight the thing came down through the forest opposite, across the brook, and stayed there on the hillside for nearly an hour.

They could hear the branches crackle as it moved about, and several times it uttered a harsh, grating, long-drawn moan, a peculiarly sinister sound. Yet it did not venture near the fire. In the morning the two trappers, after discussing the strange events of the last 36 hours, decided that they would shoulder their packs and leave the valley that afternoon. They were the more ready to do this because in spite of seeing a good deal of game sign they had caught very little fur. However it was necessary first to go along the line of their traps and gather them, and this they started out to do. All the morning they kept together, picking up trap after trap, each one empty. On first leaving camp they had the disagreeable sensation of being followed. In the dense spruce thickets they occasionally heard a branch snap after they had passed; and now and then there were slight rustling noises among the small pines to one side of them.

At noon they were back within a couple of miles of camp. In the high, bright sunlight their fears seemed absurd to the two armed men, accustomed as they were, through long years of lonely wandering in the wilderness, to face every kind of danger from man, brute or element. There were still three beaver traps to collect from a little pond in a wide ravine near by. Bauman volunteered to gather these and bring them in, while his companion went ahead to camp and made ready the packs.

On reaching the pond Bauman found three beavers in the traps, one of which had been pulled loose and carried into a beaver house. He took several hours in securing and preparing the beaver, and when he started homewards he marked, with some uneasiness, how low the sun was getting. As he hurried toward camp, under the tall trees, the silence and desolation of the forest weighted on him. His feet made no sound on the pine needles and the slanting sunrays, striking through among the straight trunks, made a gray twilight in which objects at a distance glimmered indistinctly. There was nothing to break the gloomy stillness which, when there is no breeze, always broods over these somber primeval forests. At last he came to the edge of the little glade where the camp lay and shouted as he approached it, but got no answer. The campfire had gone out, though the thin blue smoke was still curling upwards. Near it lay the packs wrapped and arranged. At first Bauman could see nobody; nor did he receive an answer to his call. Stepping forward he again shouted, and as he did so his eye fell on the body of his friend, stretched beside the trunk of a great fallen spruce. Rushing towards it the horrified trapper found that the body was still warm, but that the neck was broken, while there were four great fang marks in the throat. The footprints of the unknown beast-creature, printed deep in the soft soil, told the whole story. The unfortunate man, having finished his packing, had sat down on the spruce log with his face to the fire, and his back to the dense woods, to wait for his companion. While thus waiting, his monstrous assailant, which must have been lurking in the woods, waiting for a chance to catch one of the adventurers unprepared, came silently up from behind, walking with long noiseless steps and seemingly still on two legs. Evidently unheard, it reached the man, and broke his neck by wrenching his head back with its fore paws, while it buried its teeth in his throat. It had not eaten the body, but apparently had romped and gamboled around it in uncouth, ferocious glee, occasionally rolling over and over it; and had then fled back into the soundless depths of the woods.

Bauman, utterly unnerved and believing that the creature with which he had to deal was something either half human or half devil, some great goblin-beast, abandoned everything but his rifle and struck off at speed down the pass, not halting until he reached the beaver meadows where the hobbled ponies were still grazing. Mounting, he rode onwards through the night, until beyond reach of pursuit.

Character and Success

This article, first appearing in "The Outlook", March 31, 1900 offers some of TR's strong opinions on what was necessary for a vital and healthy political, social and individual life.

A YEAR or two ago I was speaking to a famous Yale professor, one of the most noted scholars in the country, and one who is even more than a scholar, because he is in every sense of the word a man. We had been discussing the Yale-Harvard football teams, and he remarked of a certain player: "I told them not to take him, for he was slack in his studies, and my experience is that, as a rule, the man who is slack in his studies will be slack in his foot-ball work; it is character that counts in both."

Bodily vigor is good, and vigor of intellect is even better, but far above both is character. It is true, of course, that a genius may, on certain lines, do more than a brave and manly fellow who is not a genius; and so, in sports, vast physical strength may overcome weakness, even though the puny body may have in it the heart of a lion. But, in the long run, in the great battle of life, no brilliancy of intellect, no perfection of bodily development, will count when weighed in the balance against that assemblage of virtues, active and passive, of moral qualities, which we group together under the name of character; and if between any two contestants, even in college sport or in college work, the difference in character on the right side is as great as the difference of intellect or strength the other way, it is the character side that will win.

Of course this does not mean that either intellect or bodily vigor can safely be neglected. On the contrary, it means that both should be developed, and that not the least of the benefits of developing both comes from the indirect effect which this development itself has upon the character. In very rude and ignorant communities all schooling is more or less looked down upon; but there are now very few places indeed in the United States where elementary schooling is not considered a necessity. There are any number of men, however, priding themselves upon being "hard-headed" and "practical," who sneer at book-learning and at every form of higher education, under the impression that the additional mental culture is at best useless, and is ordinarily harmful in practical life.

Not long ago two of the wealthiest men in the United States publicly committed themselves to the proposition that to go to college was a positive disadvantage for a young man who strove for success. Now, of course, the very most successful men we have ever had, men like Lincoln, had no chance to go to college, but did have such indomitable tenacity and such keen appreciation of the value of wisdom that they set to work and learned for themselves far more than they could have been taught in any academy. On the other hand, boys of weak fiber, who go to high school or college instead of going to work after getting through the primary schools, may be seriously damaged instead of benefited. But, as a rule, if the boy has in him the right stuff, it is a great advantage to him should his circumstances be so fortunate as to enable him to get the years of additional mental training. The trouble with the two rich men whose views are above quoted was that, owing largely perhaps to their own defects in early training, they did not know what success really was. Their speeches merely betrayed their own limitations, and did not furnish any argument against education. Success must always include, as its first element, earning a competence for the support of the man himself, and for the bringing up of those dependent upon him. In the vast majority of cases it ought to include financially rather more than this. But the acquisition of wealth is not in the least the only test of success. After a certain amount of wealth has been accumulated, the accumulation of more is of very little consequence indeed from the standpoint of success, as success should be understood both by the community and the individual. Wealthy men who use their wealth aright are a great power for good in the community, and help to upbuild that material national prosperity which must underlie national greatness; but if this were the only kind of success, the nation would be indeed poorly off. Successful statesmen, soldiers, sailors, explorers, historians, poets, and scientific men are also essential to national greatness, and, in fact, very much more essential than any mere successful business man can possibly be. The average man, into whom the average boy develops, is, of course, not going to be a marvel in any line, but, if he only chooses to try, he can be very good in any line, and the chances of his doing good work are immensely increased if he has trained his mind. Of course, if, as a result of his high-school, academy, or college experience, he gets to thinking that the only kind of learning is that to be found in books, he will do very little; but if he keeps his mental balance—that is, if he shows character—he will understand both what learning can do and what it cannot, and he will be all the better the more he can get.

A good deal the same thing is true of bodily development. Exactly as one kind of man sneers at college work because he does not think it bears any immediate fruit in money-getting, so another type of man sneers at college sports because he does not see their immediate effect for good in practical life. Of course, if they are carried to an excessive degree, they are altogether bad. It is a good thing for a boy to have captained his school or college eleven, but it is a very bad thing if, twenty years afterward, all that can be said of him is that he has continued to take an interest in foot-ball, base-ball, or boxing, and has with him the memory that he was once captain. A very acute observer has pointed out that, not impossibly, excessive devotion to sports and games has proved a serious detriment in the British army, by leading the officers and even the men to neglect the hard, practical work of their profession for the sake of racing, foot-ball, base-ball, polo, and tennis—until they received a very rude awakening at the hands of the Boers. Of course this means merely that any healthy pursuit can be abused. The student in a college who "crams" in order to stand at the head of his class, and neglects his health and stunts his development by working for high marks, may do himself much damage; but all that he proves is that the abuse of study is wrong. The fact remains that the study itself is essential. So it is with vigorous pastimes. If rowing or foot-ball or base-ball is treated as the end of life by any considerable section of a community, then that community shows itself to be in an unhealthy condition. If treated as it should be,—that is, as good, healthy play,—it is of great benefit, not only to the body, but in its effect upon character. To study hard implies character in the student, and to work hard at a sport which entails severe physical exertion and steady training also implies character.

All kinds of qualities go to make up character, for, emphatically, the term should include the positive no less than the negative virtues. If we say of a boy or a man, "He is of good character," we mean that he does not do a great many things that are wrong, and we also mean that he does do a great many things which imply much effort of will and readiness to face what is disagreeable. He must not steal, he must not be intemperate, he must not be vicious in any way; he must not be mean or brutal; he must not bully the weak. In fact, he must refrain from whatever is evil. But besides refraining from evil, he must do good. He must be brave and energetic; he must be resolute and persevering. The Bible always inculcates the need of the positive no less than the negative virtues, although certain people who profess to teach Christianity are apt to dwell wholly on the negative. We are bidden not merely to be harmless as doves, but also as wise as serpents. It is very much easier to carry out the former part of the order than the latter; while, on the other hand, it is of much more importance for the good of mankind that our goodness should be accompanied by wisdom than that we should merely be harmless. If with the serpent wisdom we unite the serpent guile, terrible will be the damage we do; and if, with the best of intentions, we can only manage to deserve the epithet of "harmless," it is hardly worth while to have lived in the world at all.

Perhaps there is no more important component of character than steadfast resolution. The boy who is going to make a great man, or is going to count in any way in after life, must make up his mind not merely to overcome a thousand obstacles, but to win in spite of a thousand repulses or defeats. He may be able to wrest success along the lines on which he originally started. He may have to try something entirely new. On the one hand, he must not be volatile and irresolute, and, on the other hand, he must not fear to try a new line because he has failed in another. Grant did well as a boy and well as a young man; then came a period of trouble and failure, and then the Civil War and his opportunity; and he grasped it, and rose until his name is among the greatest in our history. Young Lincoln, struggling against incalculable odds, worked his way up, trying one thing and another until he, too, struck out boldly into the turbulent torrent of our national life, at a time when only the boldest and wisest could so carry themselves as to win success and honor; and from the struggle he won both death and honor, and stands forevermore among the greatest of mankind.

Character is shown in peace no less than in war. As the greatest fertility of invention, the greatest perfection of armament, will not make soldiers out of cowards, so no mental training and no bodily vigor will make a nation great if it lacks the fundamental principles of honesty and moral cleanliness. After the death of Alexander the Great nearly all of the then civilized world was divided among the Greek monarchies ruled by his companions and their successors. This Greek world was very brilliant and very wealthy. It contained haughty military empires, and huge trading cities, under republican government, which attained the highest pitch of commercial and industrial prosperity. Art flourished to an extraordinary degree; science advanced as never before. There were academies for men of letters; there were many orators, many philosophers. Merchants and business men throve apace, and for a long period the Greek soldiers kept the superiority and renown they had won under the mighty conqueror of the East. But the heart of the people was incurably false, incurably treacherous and debased. Almost every statesman had his price, almost every soldier was a mercenary who, for a sufficient inducement, would betray any cause. Moral corruption ate into the whole social and domestic fabric, until, a little more than a century after the death of Alexander, the empire which he had left had become a mere glittering shell, which went down like a house of cards on impact with the Romans; for the Romans, with all their faults, were then a thoroughly manly race—a race of strong, virile character. Alike for the nation and the individual, the one indispensable requisite is character—character that does and dares as well as endures, character that is active in the performance of virtue no less than firm in the refusal to do aught that is vicious or degraded.

The American Boy

Originally published In "St. Nicholas," May, 1900, Roosevelt offers his thoughts on how the ideal American boy becomes the "good American man", closing with a reference to football, exhorting his readers to *"Hit the line hard; don't foul and don't shirk, but hit the line hard!"*

OF course what we have a right to expect of the American boy is that he shall turn out to be a good American man. Now, the chances are strong that he won't be much of a man unless he is a good deal of a boy. He must not be a coward or a weakling, a bully, a shirk, or a prig. He must work hard and play hard. He must be clean-minded and clean-lived, and able to hold his own under all circumstances and against all comers. It is only on these conditions that he will grow into the kind of American man of whom America can be really proud

There are always in life countless tendencies for good and for evil, and each succeeding generation sees some of these tendencies strengthened and some weakened; nor is it by any means always, alas! that the tendencies for evil are weakened and those for good strengthened. But during the last few decades there certainly have been some notable changes for good in boy life. The great growth in the love of athletic sports, for instance, while fraught with danger if it becomes one-sided and unhealthy, has beyond all question had an excellent effect in increased manliness. Forty or fifty years ago the writer on American morals was sure to deplore the effeminacy and luxury of young Americans who were born of rich parents. The boy who was well off then, especially in the big Eastern cities, lived too luxuriously, took to billiards as his chief innocent recreation, and felt small shame in his inability to take part in rough pastimes and field-sports. Nowadays, whatever other faults the son of rich parents may tend to develop, he is at least forced by the opinion of all his associates of his own age to bear himself well in manly exercises and to develop his body— and therefore, to a certain extent, his character—in the rough sports which call for pluck, endurance, and physical address.

Of course boys who live under such fortunate conditions that they have to do either a good deal of outdoor work or a good deal of what might be called natural outdoor play do not need this athletic development. In the Civil War the soldiers who came from the prairie and the backwoods and the rugged farms where stumps still dotted the clearings, and who had learned to ride in their infancy, to shoot as soon as they could handle a rifle, and to camp out whenever they got the chance, were better fitted for military work than any set of mere school or college athletes could possibly be. Moreover, to mis-estimate athletics is equally bad whether their importance is magnified or minimized. The Greeks were famous athletes, and as long as their athletic training had a normal place in their lives, it was a good thing. But it was a very bad thing when they kept up their athletic games while letting the stern qualities of soldiership and statesmanship sink into disuse.

Some of the younger readers of this book will certainly sometime read the famous letters of the younger Pliny, a Roman who wrote, with what seems to us a curiously modern touch, in the first century of the present era. His correspondence with the Emperor Trajan is particularly interesting; and not the least noteworthy thing in it is the tone of contempt with which he speaks of the Greek athletic sports, treating them as the diversions of an unwarlike people which it was safe to encourage in order to keep the Greeks from turning into anything formidable. So at one time the Persian kings had to forbid polo, because soldiers neglected their proper duties for the fascinations of the game. We cannot expect the best work from soldiers who have carried to an unhealthy extreme the sports and pastimes which would be healthy if indulged in with moderation, and have neglected to learn as they should the business of their profession. A soldier needs to know how to shoot and take cover and shift for himself—not to box or play foot-ball. There is, of course, always the risk of thus mistaking means for ends. Fox-hunting is a first-class sport; but one of the most absurd things in real life is to note the bated breath with which certain excellent fox-hunters, otherwise of quite healthy minds, speak of this admirable but not over-important pastime. They tend to make it almost as much of a fetish as, in the last century, the French and German nobles made the chase of the stag, when they carried hunting and game-preserving to a point which was ruinous to the national life. Fox-hunting is very good as a pastime, but it is about as poor a business as can be followed by any man of intelligence. Certain writers about it are fond of quoting the anecdote of a fox-hunter who, in the days of the English civil war, was discovered pursuing his favorite sport just before a great battle between the Cavaliers and the Puritans, and right between their lines as they came together. These writers apparently consider it a merit in this man that when his country was in a death-grapple, instead of taking arms and hurrying to the defense of the cause he believed right, he should placidly have gone about his usual sports. Of course, in reality the chief serious use of fox-hunting is to encourage manliness and vigor, and to keep men hardy, so that at need they can show themselves fit to take part in work or strife for their native land. When a man so far confuses ends and means as to think that fox-hunting, or polo, or foot-ball, or whatever else the sport may be, is to be itself taken as the end, instead of as the mere means of preparation to do work that counts when the time arises, when the occasion calls—why, that man had better abandon sport altogether.

No boy can afford to neglect his work, and with a boy work, as a rule, means study. Of course there are occasionally brilliant successes in life where the man has been worthless as a student when a boy. To take these exceptions as examples would be as unsafe as it would be to advocate blindness because some blind men have won undying honor by triumphing over their physical infirmity and accomplishing great results in the world. I am no advocate of senseless and excessive cramming in studies, but a boy should work, and should work hard, at his lessons—in the first place, for the sake of what he will learn, and in the next place, for the sake of the effect upon his own character of resolutely settling down to learn it. Shiftlessness, slackness, indifference in studying, are almost certain to mean inability to get on in other walks of life. Of course, as a boy grows older it is a good thing if he can shape his studies in the direction toward which he has a natural bent; but whether he can do this or not, he must put his whole heart into them. I do not believe in mischief-doing in school hours, or in the kind of animal spirits that results in making bad scholars; and I believe that those boys who take part in rough, hard play outside of school will not find any need for horse-play in school. While they study they should study just as hard as they play foot-ball in a match game. It is wise to obey the homely old adage, "Work while you work; play while you play."

A boy needs both physical and moral courage. Neither can take the place of the other. When boys become men they will find out that there are some soldiers very brave in the field who have proved timid and worthless as politicians, and some politicians who show an entire readiness to take chances and assume responsibilities in civil affairs, but who lack the fighting edge when opposed to physical danger. In each case, with soldiers and politicians alike, there is but half a virtue. The possession of the courage of the soldier does not excuse the lack of courage in the statesman and, even less does the possession of the courage of the statesman excuse shrinking on the field of battle. Now, this is all just as true of boys. A coward who will take a blow without returning it is a contemptible creature; but, after all, he is hardly as contemptible as the boy who dares not stand up for what he deems right against the sneers of his companions who are themselves wrong. Ridicule is one of the favorite weapons of wickedness, and it is sometimes incomprehensible how good and brave boys will be influenced for evil by the jeers of associates who have no one quality that calls for respect, but who affect to laugh at the very traits which ought to be peculiarly the cause for pride.

There is no need to be a prig. There is no need for a boy to preach about his own good conduct and virtue. If he does he will make himself offensive and ridiculous. But there is urgent need that he should practise decency; that he should be clean and straight, honest and truthful, gentle and tender, as well as brave. If he can once get to a proper understanding of things, he will have a far more hearty contempt for the boy who has begun a course of feeble dissipation, or who is untruthful, or mean, or dishonest, or cruel, than this boy and his fellows can possibly, in return, feel for him. The very fact that the boy should be manly and able to hold his own, that he should be ashamed to submit to bullying without instant retaliation, should, in return, make him abhor any form of bullying, cruelty, or brutality.

There are two delightful books, Thomas Hughes's "Tom Brown at Rugby," and Aldrich's "Story of a Bad Boy," which I hope every boy still reads; and I think American boys will always feel more in sympathy with Aldrich's story, because there is in it none of the fagging, and the bullying which goes with fagging, the account of which, and the acceptance of which, always puzzle an American admirer of Tom Brown.

There is the same contrast between two stories of Kipling's. One, called "Captains Courageous," describes in the liveliest way just what a boy should be and do. The hero is painted in the beginning as the spoiled, over-indulged child of wealthy parents, of a type which we do sometimes unfortunately see, and than which there exist few things more objectionable on the face of the broad earth. This boy is afterward thrown on his own resources, amid wholesome surroundings, and is forced to work hard among boys and men who are real boys and real men doing real work. The effect is invaluable. On the other hand, if one wishes to find types of boys to be avoided with utter dislike, one will find them in another story by Kipling, called "Stalky & Co.," a story which ought never to have been written, for there is hardly a single form of meanness which it does not seem to extol, or of school mismanagement which it does not seem to applaud. Bullies do not make brave men; and boys or men of foul life cannot become good citizens, good Americans, until they change; and even after the change scars will be left on their souls.

The boy can best become a good man by being a good boy—not a goody-goody boy, but just a plain good boy. I do not mean that he must love only the negative virtues; I mean he must love the positive virtues also. "Good," in the largest sense, should include whatever is fine, straightforward, clean, brave, and manly. The best boys I know—the best men I know—are good at their studies or their business, fearless and stalwart, hated and feared by all that is wicked and depraved, incapable of submitting to wrong-doing, and equally incapable of being aught but tender to the weak and helpless. A healthy-minded boy should feel hearty contempt for the coward, and even more hearty indignation for the boy who bullies girls or small boys, or tortures animals. One prime reason for abhorring cowards is because every good boy should have it in him to thrash the objectionable boy as the need arises.

Of course the effect that a thoroughly manly, thoroughly straight and upright boy can have upon the companions of his own age, and upon those who are younger, is incalculable. If he is not thoroughly manly, then they will not respect him, and his good qualities will count for but little; while, of course, if he is mean, cruel, or wicked, then his physical strength and force of mind merely make him so much the more objectionable a member of society. He cannot do good work if he is not strong and does not try with his whole heart and soul to count in any contest; and his strength will be a curse to himself and to every one else if he does not have thorough command over himself and over his own evil passions, and if he does not use his strength on the side of decency, justice, and fair dealing.

In short, in life, as in a foot-ball game, the principle to follow is:

Hit the line hard;
don't foul and don't shirk,
but hit the line hard!

Diary Pages from February, 1884

On February 14, 1884, Roosevelt's his wife and mother died within hours of one another in the Roosevelt house in New York City. His mother, Martha Bulloch Roosevelt age 50, succumbed to typhus, and his wife Alice Lee Roosevelt, age 22, died giving birth to her namesake.

February, Thursday 14. 1884
X
The light has gone out of my life

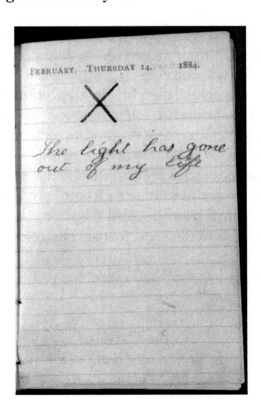

February, Friday 15. 1884
(blank)

February, Saturday 16. 1884
Alice Hathaway Lee, Born at Chestnut Hill, July 29th 1861. I saw her first on Oct 1878; I wooed her for over a year before I won her; we were betrothed on Jan 25th 1880, and it was announced on Feb 16th; on Oct 27th of the same year we were married; we spent three years of happiness greater and more unalloyed than I have ever known fall to the lot of others; on Feb 14th 1884

February, Sunday 17. 1884
her baby was born and on Feb 14th she died in my arms. As my mother had died in the same house on the same day, but a few hours previously. On Feb 16th they were buried together in Greenwood.

On Feb 17th I christened the baby Alice Lee Roosevelt

For joy or for sorrow my life has now been lived out.

The Strenuous Life

Among other things, Roosevelt was known for his "cowboy" persona. In this commentary is from an April 10, 1899 speech given to the Hamilton Club in Chicago, IL he extols the virtues being a man "who does not shrink from danger, from hardship, or from bitter toil".

IN speaking to you, men of the greatest city of the West, men of the State which gave to the country Lincoln and Grant, men who preeminently and distinctly embody all that is most American in the American character, I wish to preach, not the doctrine of ignoble ease, but the doctrine of the strenuous life, the life of toil and effort, of labor and strife; to preach that highest form of success which comes, not to the man who desires mere easy peace, but to the man who does not shrink from danger, from hardship, or from bitter toil, and who out of these wins the splendid ultimate triumph.

A life of slothful ease, a life of that peace which springs merely from lack either of desire or of power to strive after great things, is as little worthy of a nation as of an individual. I ask only that what every self-respecting American demands from himself and from his sons shall be demanded of the American nation as a whole. Who among you would teach your boys that ease, that peace, is to be the first consideration in their eyes— to be the ultimate goal after which they strive? You men of Chicago have made this city great, you men of Illinois have done your share, and more than your share, in making

America great, because you neither preach nor practise such a doctrine. You work yourselves, and you bring up your sons to work. If you are rich and are worth your salt, you will teach your sons that though they may have leisure, it is not to be spent in idleness; for wisely used leisure merely means that those who possess it, being free from the necessity of working for their livelihood, are all the more bound to carry on some kind of non-remunerative work in science, in letters, in art, in exploration, in historical research—work of the type we most need in this country, the successful carrying out of which reflects most honor upon the nation.

We do not admire the man of timid peace. We admire the man who embodies victorious effort; the man who never wrongs his neighbor, who is prompt to help a friend, but who has those virile qualities necessary to win in the stern strife of actual life.

It is hard to fail, but it is worse never to have tried to succeed. In this life we get nothing save by effort. Freedom from effort in the present merely means that there has been stored up effort in the past. A man can be freed from the necessity of work only by the fact that he or his fathers before him have worked to good purpose. If the freedom thus purchased is used aright, and the man still does actual work, though of a different kind, whether as a writer or a general, whether in the field of politics or in the field of exploration and adventure, he shows he deserves his good fortune. But if he treats this period of freedom from the need of actual labor as a period, not of preparation, but of mere enjoyment, even though perhaps not of vicious enjoyment, he shows that he is simply a cumberer of the earth's surface, and he surely unfits himself to hold his own with his fellows if the need to do so should again arise. A mere life of ease is not in the end a very satisfactory life, and, above all, it is a life which ultimately unfits those who follow it for serious work in the world.

In the last analysis a healthy state can exist only when the men and women who make it up lead clean, vigorous, healthy lives; when the children are so trained that they shall endeavor, not to shirk difficulties, but to overcome them; not to seek ease, but to know how to wrest triumph from toil and risk. The man must be glad to do a man's work, to dare and endure and to labor; to keep himself, and to keep those dependent upon him. The woman must be the housewife, the helpmeet of the homemaker, the wise and fearless mother of many healthy children. In one of Daudet's powerful and melancholy books he speaks of "the fear of maternity, the haunting terror of the young wife of the present day." When such words can be truthfully written of a nation, that nation is rotten to the heart's core. When men fear work or fear righteous war, when women fear motherhood, they tremble on the brink of doom; and well it is that they should vanish from the earth, where they are fit subjects for the scorn of all men and women who are themselves strong and brave and high-minded.

As it is with the individual, so it is with the nation. It is a base untruth to say that happy is the nation that has no history. Thrice happy is the nation that has a glorious history. Far better it is to dare mighty things, to win glorious triumphs, even though checkered by failure, than to take rank with those poor spirits who neither enjoy much nor suffer much, because they live in the gray twilight that knows not victory nor defeat. If in 1861 the men who loved the Union had believed that peace was the end of all things, and war and strife the worst of all things, and had acted up to their belief, we would have saved hundreds of thousands of lives, we would have saved hundreds of millions of dollars. Moreover, besides saving all the blood and treasure we then lavished, we would have prevented the heartbreak of many women, the dissolution of many homes, and we would have spared the country those months of gloom and shame when it seemed as if our armies marched only to defeat. We could have avoided all this suffering simply by shrinking from strife. And if we had thus avoided it, we would have shown that we were weaklings, and that we were unfit to stand among the great nations of the earth. Thank God for the iron in the blood of our fathers, the men who upheld the wisdom of Lincoln, and bore sword or rifle in the armies of Grant! Let us, the children of the men who proved themselves equal to the mighty days, let us, the children of the men who carried the great Civil War to a triumphant conclusion, praise the God of our fathers that the ignoble counsels of peace were rejected; that the suffering and loss, the blackness of sorrow and despair, were unflinchingly faced, and the years of strife endured; for in the end the slave was freed, the Union restored, and the mighty American republic placed once more as a helmeted queen among nations.

We of this generation do not have to face a task such as that our fathers faced, but we have our tasks, and woe to us if we fail to perform them! We cannot, if we would, play the part of China, and be content to rot by inches in ignoble ease within our borders, taking no interest in what goes on beyond them, sunk in a scrambling commercialism; heedless of the higher life, the life of aspiration, of toil and risk, busying ourselves only with the wants of our bodies for the day, until suddenly we should find, beyond a shadow of question, what China has already found, that in this world the nation that has trained itself to a career of unwarlike and isolated ease is bound, in the end, to go down before other nations which have not lost the manly and adventurous qualities. If we are to be a really great people, we must strive in good faith to play a great part in the world. We cannot avoid meeting great issues. All that we can determine for ourselves is whether we shall meet them well or ill. In 1898 we could not help being brought face to face with the problem of war with Spain. All we could decide was whether we should shrink like cowards from the contest, or enter into it as beseemed a brave and high-spirited people; and, once in, whether failure or success should crown our banners. So it is now. We cannot avoid the responsibilities that confront us in Hawaii, Cuba, Puerto Rico, and the Philippines. All we can decide is whether we shall meet them in a way that will redound to the national credit, or whether we shall make of our dealings with these new problems a dark and shameful page in our history. To refuse to deal with them at all merely amounts to dealing with them badly. We have a given problem to solve. If we undertake the solution, there is, of course, always danger that we may not solve it aright; but to refuse to undertake the solution simply renders it certain that we cannot possibly solve it aright. The timid man, the lazy man, the man who distrusts his country, the over-civilized man, who has lost the great fighting, masterful virtues, the ignorant man, and the man of dull mind, whose soul is incapable of feeling the mighty lift that thrills "stern men with empires in their brains"—all these, of course, shrink from seeing the nation undertake its new duties; shrink from seeing us build a navy and an army adequate to our needs; shrink from seeing us do our share of the world's work, by bringing order out of chaos in the great, fair tropic islands from which the valor of our soldiers and sailors has driven the Spanish flag. These are the men who fear the strenuous life, who fear the only national life which is really worth leading. They believe in that cloistered life which saps the hardy virtues in a nation, as it saps them in the individual; or else they are wedded to that base spirit of gain and greed which recognizes in commercialism the be-all and end-all of national life, instead of realizing that, though an indispensable element, it is, after all, but one of the many elements that go to make up true national greatness. No country can long endure if its foundations are not laid deep in the material prosperity which comes from thrift, from business energy and enterprise, from hard, unsparing effort in the fields of industrial activity; but neither was any nation ever yet truly great if it relied upon material prosperity alone. All honor must be paid to the architects of our material prosperity, to the great captains of industry who have built our factories and our railroads, to the strong men who toil for wealth with brain or hand; for great is the debt of the nation to these and their kind. But our debt is yet greater to the men whose highest type is to be found in a statesman like Lincoln, a soldier like Grant. They showed by their lives that they recognized the law of work, the law of strife; they toiled to win a competence for themselves and those dependent upon them; but they recognized that there were yet other and even loftier duties—duties to the nation and duties to the race.

We cannot sit huddled within our own borders and avow ourselves merely an assemblage of well-to-do hucksters who care nothing for what happens beyond. Such a policy would defeat even its own end; for as the nations grow to have ever wider and wider interests, and are brought into closer and closer contact, if we are to hold our own in the struggle for naval and commercial supremacy, we must build up our power without our own borders. We must build the isthmian canal, and we must grasp the points of vantage which will enable us to have our say in deciding the destiny of the oceans of the East and the West.

So much for the commercial side. From the standpoint of international honor the argument is even stronger. The guns that thundered off Manila and Santiago left us echoes of glory, but they also left us a legacy of duty. If we drove out a medieval tyranny only to make room for savage anarchy, we had better not have begun the task at all. It is worse than idle to say that we have no duty to perform, and can leave to their fates the islands we have conquered. Such a course would be the course of infamy. It would be followed at once by utter chaos in the wretched islands themselves. Some stronger, manlier power would have to step in and do the work, and we would have shown ourselves weaklings, unable to carry to successful completion the labors that great and high-spirited nations are eager to undertake.

The work must be done; we cannot escape our responsibility; and if we are worth our salt, we shall be glad of the chance to do the work—glad of the chance to show ourselves equal to one of the great tasks set modern civilization. But let us not deceive ourselves as to the importance of the task. Let us not be misled by vainglory into underestimating the strain it will put on our powers. Above all, let us, as we value our own self-respect, face the responsibilities with proper seriousness, courage, and high resolve. We must demand the highest order of integrity and ability in our public men who are to grapple with these new problems. We must hold to a rigid accountability those public servants who show unfaithfulness to the interests of the nation or inability to rise to the high level of the new demands upon our strength and our resources.

Of course we must remember not to judge any public servant by any one act, and especially should we beware of attacking the men who are merely the occasions and not the causes of disaster. Let me illustrate what I mean by the army and the navy. If twenty years ago we had gone to war, we should have found the navy as absolutely unprepared as the army. At that time our ships could not have encountered with success the fleets of Spain any more than nowadays we can put untrained soldiers, no matter how brave, who are armed with archaic black-powder weapons, against well-drilled regulars armed with the highest type of modern repeating rifle. But in the early eighties the attention of the nation became directed to our naval needs. Congress most wisely made a series of appropriations to build up a new navy, and under a succession of able and patriotic secretaries, of both political parties, the navy was gradually built up, until its material became equal to its splendid personnel, with the result that in the summer of 1898 it leaped to its proper place as one of the most brilliant and formidable fighting navies in the entire world. We rightly pay all honor to the men controlling the navy at the time it won these great deeds, honor to Secretary Long and Admiral Dewey, to the captains who handled the ships in action, to the daring lieutenants who braved death in the smaller craft, and to the heads of bureaus at Washington who saw that the ships were so commanded, so armed, so equipped, so well engined, as to insure the best results. But let us also keep ever in mind that all of this would not have availed if it had not been for the wisdom of the men who during the preceding fifteen years had built up the navy. Keep in mind the secretaries of the navy during those years; keep in mind the senators and congressmen who by their votes gave the money necessary to build and to armor the ships, to construct the great guns, and to train the crews; remember also those who actually did build the ships, the armor, and the guns; and remember the admirals and captains who handled battle-ship, cruiser, and torpedo-boat on the high seas, alone and in squadrons, developing the seamanship, the gunnery, and the power of acting together, which their successors utilized so gloriously at Manila and off Santiago.

And, gentlemen, remember the converse, too. Remember that justice has two sides. Be just to those who built up the navy, and, for the sake of the future of the country, keep in mind those who opposed its building up. Read the "Congressional Record." Find out the senators and congressmen who opposed the grants for building the new ships; who opposed the purchase of armor, without which the ships were worthless; who opposed any adequate maintenance for the Navy Department, and strove to cut down the number of men necessary to man our fleets. The men who did these things were one and all working to bring disaster on the country. They have no share in the glory of Manila, in the honor of Santiago. They have no cause to feel proud of the valor of our sea-captains, of the renown of our flag. Their motives may or may not have been good, but their acts were heavily fraught with evil. They did ill for the national honor, and we won in spite of their sinister opposition.

Now, apply all this to our public men of to-day. Our army has never been built up as it should be built up. I shall not discuss with an audience like this the puerile suggestion that a nation of seventy millions of freemen is in danger of losing its liberties from the existence of an army of one hundred thousand men, three fourths of whom will be employed in certain foreign islands, in certain coast fortresses, and on Indian reservations. No man of good sense and stout heart can take such a proposition seriously. If we are such weaklings as the proposition implies, then we are unworthy of freedom in any event. To no body of men in the United States is the country so much indebted as to the splendid officers and enlisted men of the regular army and navy. There is no body from which the country has less to fear, and none of which it should be prouder, none which it should be more anxious to upbuild.

Our army needs complete reorganization—not merely enlarging—and the reorganization can only come as the result of legislation. A proper general staff should be established, and the positions of ordnance, commissary, and quartermaster officers should be filled by detail from the line. Above all, the army must be given the chance to exercise in large bodies. Never again should we see, as we saw in the Spanish war, major-generals in command of divisions who had never before commanded three companies together in the field. Yet, incredible to relate, Congress has shown a queer inability to learn some of the lessons of the war. There were large bodies of men in both branches who opposed the declaration of war, who opposed the ratification of peace, who opposed the upbuilding of the army, and who even opposed the purchase of armor at a reasonable price for the battle-ships and cruisers, thereby putting an absolute stop to the building of any new fighting-ships for the navy. If, during the years to come, any disaster should befall our arms, afloat or ashore, and thereby any shame come to the United States, remember that the blame will lie upon the men whose names appear upon the roll-calls of Congress on the wrong side of these great questions. On them will lie the burden of any loss of our soldiers and sailors, of any dishonor to the flag; and upon you and the people of this country will lie the blame if you do not repudiate, in no unmistakable way, what these men have done. The blame will not rest upon the untrained commander of untried troops, upon the civil officers of a department the organization of which has been left utterly inadequate, or upon the admiral with an insufficient number of ships; but upon the public men who have so lamentably failed in forethought as to refuse to remedy these evils long in advance, and upon the nation that stands behind those public men.

So, at the present hour, no small share of the responsibility for the blood shed in the Philippines, the blood of our brothers, and the blood of their wild and ignorant foes, lies at the thresholds of those who so long delayed the adoption of the treaty of peace, and of those who by their worse than foolish words deliberately invited a savage people to plunge into a war fraught with sure disaster for them—a war, too, in which our own brave men who follow the flag must pay with their blood for the silly, mock humanitarianism of the prattlers who sit at home in peace.

The army and the navy are the sword and the shield which this nation must carry if she is to do her duty among the nations of the earth—if she is not to stand merely as the China of the western hemisphere. Our proper conduct toward the tropic islands we have wrested from Spain is merely the form which our duty has taken at the moment. Of course we are bound to handle the affairs of our own household well. We must see that there is civic honesty, civic cleanliness, civic good sense in our home administration of city, State, and nation. We must strive for honesty in office, for honesty toward the creditors of the nation and of the individual; for the widest freedom of individual initiative where possible, and for the wisest control of individual initiative where it is hostile to the welfare of the many. But because we set our own household in order we are not thereby excused from playing our part in the great affairs of the world. A man's first duty is to his own home, but he is not thereby excused from doing his duty to the State; for if he fails in this second duty it is under the penalty of ceasing to be a freeman. In the same way, while a nation's first duty is within its own borders, it is not thereby absolved from facing its duties in the world as a whole; and if it refuses to do so, it merely forfeits its right to struggle for a place among the peoples that shape the destiny of mankind.

In the West Indies and the Philippines alike we are confronted by most difficult problems. It is cowardly to shrink from solving them in the proper way; for solved they must be, if not by us, then by some stronger and more manful race. If we are too weak, too selfish, or too foolish to solve them, some bolder and abler people must undertake the solution. Personally, I am far too firm a believer in the greatness of my country and the power of my countrymen to admit for one moment that we shall ever be driven to the ignoble alternative.

The problems are different for the different islands. Puerto Rico is not large enough to stand alone. We must govern it wisely and well, primarily in the interest of its own people. Cuba is, in my judgment, entitled ultimately to settle for itself whether it shall be an independent state or an integral portion of the mightiest of republics. But until order and stable liberty are secured, we must remain in the island to insure them, and infinite tact, judgment, moderation, and courage must be shown by our military and civil representatives in keeping the island pacified, in relentlessly stamping out brigandage, in protecting all alike, and yet in showing proper recognition to the men who have fought for Cuban liberty. The Philippines offer a yet graver problem. Their population includes half-caste and native Christians, warlike Moslems, and wild pagans. Many of their people are utterly unfit for self-government, and show no signs of becoming fit. Others may in time become fit but at present can only take part in self-government under a wise supervision, at once firm and beneficent. We have driven Spanish tyranny from the islands.

If we now let it be replaced by savage anarchy, our work has been for harm and not for good. I have scant patience with those who fear to undertake the task of governing the Philippines, and who openly avow that they do fear to undertake it, or that they shrink from it because of the expense and trouble; but I have even scanter patience with those who make a pretense of humanitarianism to hide and cover their timidity, and who cant about "liberty" and the "consent of the governed," in order to excuse themselves for their unwillingness to play the part of men. Their doctrines, if carried out, would make it incumbent upon us to leave the Apaches of Arizona to work out their own salvation, and to decline to interfere in a single Indian reservation. Their doctrines condemn your forefathers and mine for ever having settled in these United States.

England's rule in India and Egypt has been of great benefit to England, for it has trained up generations of men accustomed to look at the larger and loftier side of public life. It has been of even greater benefit to India and Egypt. And finally, and most of all, it has advanced the cause of civilization. So, if we do our duty aright in the Philippines, we will add to that national renown which is the highest and finest part of national life, will greatly benefit the people of the Philippine Islands, and, above all, we will play our part well in the great work of uplifting mankind. But to do this work, keep ever in mind that we must show in a very high degree the qualities of courage, of honesty, and of good judgment. Resistance must be stamped out. The first and all-important work to be done is to establish the supremacy of our flag. We must put down armed resistance before we can accomplish anything else, and there should be no parleying, no faltering, in dealing with our foe. As for those in our own country who encourage the foe, we can afford contemptuously to disregard them; but it must be remembered that their utterances are not saved from being treasonable merely by the fact that they are despicable.

When once we have put down armed resistance, when once our rule is acknowledged, then an even more difficult task will begin, for then we must see to it that the islands are administered with absolute honesty and with good judgment. If we let the public service of the islands be turned into the prey of the spoils politician, we shall have begun to tread the path which Spain trod to her own destruction. We must send out there only good and able men, chosen for their fitness, and not because of their partizan service, and these men must not only administer impartial justice to the natives and serve their own government with honesty and fidelity, but must show the utmost tact and firmness, remembering that, with such people as those with whom we are to deal, weakness is the greatest of crimes, and that next to weakness comes lack of consideration for their principles and prejudices.

I preach to you, then, my countrymen, that our country calls not for the life of ease but for the life of strenuous endeavor. The twentieth century looms before us big with the fate of many nations. If we stand idly by, if we seek merely swollen, slothful ease and ignoble peace, if we shrink from the hard contests where men must win at hazard of their lives and at the risk of all they hold dear, then the bolder and stronger peoples will pass us by, and will win for themselves the domination of the world. Let us therefore boldly face the life of strife, resolute to do our duty well and manfully; resolute to uphold righteousness by deed and by word; resolute to be both honest and brave, to serve high ideals, yet to use practical methods. Above all, let us shrink from no strife, moral or physical, within or without the nation, provided we are certain that the strife is justified, for it is only through strife, through hard and dangerous endeavor, that we shall ultimately win the goal of true national greatness.

TR's Controversial Dinner

On Oct. 16, 1901, Roosevelt invited distinguished educator and renowned African-American leader Booker T. Washington to dine with the first family at the White House. Although blacks had worked on the construction of the White House, had worked for most of the presidents, held political office, and occasionally met with the President to discuss business in his office, not a single African-American had ever been invited to dine there.

In 1901, segregation was law, and this dinner between a former slave and the President of the United States was incredibly controversial, drawing praise from some liberal whites, inspiring pride in many blacks and enraging both Southern and Northern racists.

Here is a letter from Roosevelt to Washington written a month prior to the controversial dinner:

EXECUTIVE MANSION, WASHINGTON.

Buffalo, N.Y., September 14, 1901

My dear Mr. Washington:

I write you at once to say that to my deep regret my visit south must now be given up.

When are you coming north? I must see you as soon as possible. I want to talk over the question of possible future appointments in the south exactly on the lines of our last conversation together.

I hope that my visit to Tuskegee is merely deferred for a short season.

Faithfully Yours,
Theodore Roosevelt

Booker T. Washington, Esq.,
Tuskegee, Alabama

Citizenship in a Republic
"The Man in the Arena"

This speech, emphasizing Roosevelt's belief that the success of a republic rested not on the brilliance of its citizens but on disciplined work and character, was delivered April 23, 1910 at the Sorbonne in Paris, France -- TR's famous "Man in the Arena" excerpt is in bold text.

Strange and impressive associations rise in the mind of a man from the New World who speaks before this august body in this ancient institution of learning. Before his eyes pass the shadows of mighty kings and warlike nobles, of great masters of law and theology; through the shining dust of the dead centuries he sees crowded figures that tell of the power and learning and splendor of times gone by; and he sees also the innumerable host of humble students to whom clerkship meant emancipation, to whom it was well-nigh the only outlet from the dark thraldom of the Middle Ages.

This was the most famous university of mediæval Europe at a time when no one dreamed that there was a New World to discover. Its services to the cause of human knowledge already stretched far back into the remote past at the time when my forefathers, three centuries ago, were among the sparse bands of traders, ploughmen, wood-choppers, and fisherfolk who, in hard struggle with the iron unfriendliness of the Indian-haunted land, were laying the foundations of what has now become the giant republic of the West. To conquer a continent, to tame the shaggy roughness of wild nature, means grim warfare; and the generations engaged in it can not keep, still less add to, the stores of garnered wisdom which once were theirs, and which are still in the hands of their brethren who dwell in the old land. To conquer the wilderness means to wrest victory from the same hostile forces with which mankind struggled in the immemorial infancy of our race. The primeval conditions must be met by primeval qualities which are incompatible with the retention of much that has been painfully acquired by humanity as through the ages it has striven upward toward civilization. In conditions so primitive there can be but a primitive culture. At first only the rudest schools can be established, for no others would meet the needs of the hard-driven, sinewy folk who thrust forward the frontier in the teeth of savage man and savage nature; and many years elapse before any of these schools can develop into seats of higher learning and broader culture.

The pioneer days pass; the stump-dotted clearings expand into vast stretches of fertile farmland; the stockaded clusters of log cabins change into towns; the hunters of game, the fellers of trees, the rude frontier traders and tillers of the soil, the men who wander all their lives long through the wilderness as the heralds and harbingers of an oncoming civilization, themselves vanish before the civilization for which they have prepared the way. The children of their successors and supplanters, and then their children and children's children, change and develop with extraordinary rapidity. The conditions accentuate vices and virtues, energy and ruthlessness, all the good qualities and all the defects of an intense individualism, self-reliant, self-centred, far more conscious of its rights than of its duties, and blind to its own shortcomings. To the hard materialism of the frontier days succeeds the hard materialism of an industrialism even more intense and absorbing than that of the older nations; although these themselves have likewise already entered on the age of a complex and predominantly industrial civilization.

As the country grows, its people, who have won success in so many lines, turn back to try to recover the possessions of the mind and the spirit, which perforce their fathers threw aside in order better to wage the first rough battles for the continent their children inherit. The leaders of thought and of action grope their way forward to a new life, realizing, sometimes dimly, sometimes clear-sightedly, that the life of material gain, whether for a nation or an individual, is of value only as a foundation, only as there is added to it the uplift that comes from devotion to loftier ideals. The new life thus sought can in part be developed afresh from what is round about in the New World; but it can be developed in full only by freely drawing upon the treasure-houses of the Old World, upon the treasures stored in the ancient abodes of wisdom and learning, such as this where I speak to-day. It is a mistake for any nation merely to copy another; but it is an even greater mistake, it is a proof of weakness in any nation, not to be anxious to learn from another, and willing and able to adapt that learning to the new national conditions and make it fruitful and productive therein. It is for us of the New World to sit at the feet of the Gamaliel of the Old; then, if we have the right stuff in us, we can show that Paul in his turn can become a teacher as well as a scholar.

To-day I shall speak to you on the subject of individual citizenship, the one subject of vital importance to you, my hearers, and to me and my countrymen, because you and we are citizens of great democratic republics. A democratic republic such as each of ours—an effort to realize in its full sense government by, of, and for the people—represents the most gigantic of all possible social experiments, the one fraught with greatest possibilities alike for good and for evil. The success of republics like yours and like ours means the glory, and our failure the despair, of mankind; and for you and for us the question of the quality of the individual citizen is supreme. Under other forms of government, under the rule of one man or of a very few men, the quality of the rulers is all-important. If, under such governments, the quality of the rulers is high enough, then the nation may for generations lead a brilliant career, and add substantially to the sum of world achievement, no matter how low the quality of the average citizen; because the average citizen is an almost negligible quantity in working out the final results of that type of national greatness.

But with you and with us the case is different. With you here, and with us in my own home, in the long run, success or failure will be conditioned upon the way in which the average man, the average woman, does his or her duty, first in the ordinary, every-day affairs of life, and next in those great occasional crises which call for the heroic virtues. The average citizen must be a good citizen if our republics are to succeed. The stream will not permanently rise higher than the main source; and the main source of national power and national greatness is found in the average citizenship of the nation. Therefore it behooves us to do our best to see that the standard of the average citizen is kept high; and the average can not be kept high unless the standard of the leaders is very much higher.

It is well if a large proportion of the leaders in any republic, in any democracy, are, as a matter of course, drawn from the classes represented in this audience to-day; but only provided that those classes possess the gifts of sympathy with plain people and of devotion to great ideals. You and those like you have received special advantages; you have all of you had the opportunity for mental training; many of you have had leisure; most of you have had a chance for the enjoyment of life far greater than comes to the majority of your fellows. To you and your kind much has been given, and from you much should be expected. Yet there are certain failings against which it is especially incumbent that both men of trained and cultivated intellect, and men of inherited wealth and position, should especially guard themselves, because to these failings they are especially liable; and if yielded to, their—your—chances of useful service are at an end.

Let the man of learning, the man of lettered leisure, beware of that queer and cheap temptation to pose to himself and to others as the cynic, as the man who has outgrown emotions and beliefs, the man to whom good and evil are as one. The poorest way to face life is to face it with a sneer. There are many men who feel a kind of twisted pride in cynicism; there are many who confine themselves to criticism of the way others do what they themselves dare not even attempt. There is no more unhealthy being, no man less worthy of respect, than he who either really holds, or feigns to hold, an attitude of sneering disbelief toward all that is great and lofty, whether in achievement or in that noble effort which, even if it fails, comes second to achievement. A cynical habit of thought and speech, a readiness to criticise work which the critic himself never tries to perform, an intellectual aloofness which will not accept contact with life's realities—all these are marks, not, as the possessor would fain think, of superiority, but of weakness. They mark the men unfit to bear their part manfully in the stern strife of living, who seek, in the affectation of contempt for the achievements of others, to hide from others and from themselves their own weakness. The rôle is easy; there is none easier, save only the rôle of the man who sneers alike at both criticism and performance.

It is not the critic who counts; not the man who points out how the strong man stumbles, or where the doer of deeds could have done them better. The credit belongs to the man who is actually in the arena, whose face is marred by dust and sweat and blood; who strives valiantly; who errs, and comes short again and again, because there is no effort without error and shortcoming; but who does actually strive to do the deeds; who knows the great enthusiasms, the great devotions; who spends himself in a worthy cause; who at the best knows in the end the triumph of high achievement, and who at the worst, if he fails, at least fails while daring greatly, so that his place shall never be with those cold and timid souls who know neither victory nor defeat. Shame on the man of cultivated taste who permits refinement to develop into a fastidiousness that unfits him for doing the rough work of a workaday world. Among the free peoples who govern themselves there is but a small field of usefulness open for the men of cloistered life who shrink from contact with their fellows. Still less room is there for those who deride or slight what is done by those who actually bear the brunt of the day; nor yet for those others who always profess that they would like to take action, if only the conditions of life were not what they actually are. The man who does nothing cuts the same sordid figure in the pages of history, whether he be cynic, or fop, or voluptuary. There is little use for the being whose tepid soul knows nothing of the great and generous emotion, of the high pride, the stern belief, the lofty enthusiasm, of the men who quell the storm and ride the thunder. Well for these men if they succeed; well also, though not so well, if they fail, given only that they have nobly ventured, and have put forth all their heart and strength. It is war-worn Hotspur, spent with hard fighting, he of the many errors and the valiant end, over whose memory we love to linger, not over the memory of the young lord who "but for the vile guns would have been a soldier."

France has taught many lessons to other nations: surely one of the most important is the lesson her whole history teaches, that a high artistic and literary development is compatible with notable leadership in arms and statecraft. The brilliant gallantry of the French soldier has for many centuries been proverbial; and during these same centuries at every court in Europe the "freemasons of fashion" have treated the French tongue as their common speech; while every artist and man of letters, and every man of science able to appreciate that marvellous instrument of precision, French prose, has turned toward France for aid and inspiration. How long the leadership in arms and letters has lasted is curiously illustrated by the fact that the earliest masterpiece in a modern tongue is the splendid French epic which tells of Roland's doom and the vengeance of Charlemagne when the lords of the Frankish host were stricken at Roncesvalles.

Let those who have, keep, let those who have not, strive to attain, a high standard of cultivation and scholarship. Yet let us remember that these stand second to certain other things. There is need of a sound body, and even more need of a sound mind. But above mind and above body stands character—the sum of those qualities which we mean when we speak of a man's force and courage, of his good faith and sense of honor.

I believe in exercise for the body, always provided that we keep in mind that physical development is a means and not an end.

I believe, of course, in giving to all the people a good education. But the education must contain much besides book-learning in order to be really good. We must ever remember that no keenness and subtleness of intellect, no polish, no cleverness, in any way make up for the lack of the great solid qualities. Self-restraint, self-mastery, common sense, the power of accepting individual responsibility and yet of acting in conjunction with others, courage and resolution—these are the qualities which mark a masterful people. Without them no people can control itself, or save itself from being controlled from the outside. I speak to a brilliant assemblage; I speak in a great university which represents the flower of the highest intellectual development; I pay all homage to intellect, and to elaborate and specialized training of the intellect; and yet I know I shall have the assent of all of you present when I add that more important still are the commonplace, every-day qualities and virtues.

Such ordinary, every-day qualities include the will and the power to work, to fight at need, and to have plenty of healthy children. The need that the average man shall work is so obvious as hardly to warrant insistence. There are a few people in every country so born that they can lead lives of leisure. These fill a useful function if they make it evident that leisure does not mean idleness; for some of the most valuable work needed by civilization is essentially non-remunerative in its character, and of course the people who do this work should in large part be drawn from those to whom remuneration is an object of indifference. But the average man must earn his own livelihood. He should be trained to do so, and he should be trained to feel that he occupies a contemptible position if he does not do so; that he is not an object of envy if he is idle, at whichever end of the social scale he stands, but an object of contempt, an object of derision.

In the next place, the good man should be both a strong and a brave man; that is, he should be able to fight, he should be able to serve his country as a soldier, if the need arises. There are well-meaning philosophers who declaim against the unrighteousness of war. They are right only if they lay all their emphasis upon the unrighteousness. War is a dreadful thing, and unjust war is a crime against humanity. But it is such a crime because it is unjust, not because it is war. The choice must ever be in favor of righteousness, and this whether the alternative be peace or whether the alternative be war. The question must not be merely, Is there to be peace or war? The question must be, Is the right to prevail? Are the great laws of righteousness once more to be fulfilled? And the answer from a strong and virile people must be, "Yes," whatever the cost. Every honorable effort should always be made to avoid war, just as every honorable effort should always be made by the individual in private life to keep out of a brawl, to keep out of trouble; but no self-respecting individual, no self-respecting nation, can or ought to submit to wrong.

Finally, even more important than ability to work, even more important than ability to fight at need, is it to remember that the chief of blessings for any nation is that it shall leave its seed to inherit the land. It was the crown of blessings in Biblical times; and it is the crown of blessings now. The greatest of all curses is the curse of sterility, and the severest of all condemnations should be that visited upon wilful sterility.

The first essential in any civilization is that the man and the woman shall be father and mother of healthy children, so that the race shall increase and not decrease. If this is not so, if through no fault of the society there is failure to increase, it is a great misfortune. If the failure is due to deliberate and wilful fault, then it is not merely a misfortune, it is one of those crimes of ease and self-indulgence, of shrinking from pain and effort and risk, which in the long run Nature punishes more heavily than any other. If we of the great republics, if we, the free people who claim to have emancipated ourselves from the thraldom of wrong and error, bring down on our heads the curse that comes upon the wilfully barren, then it will be an idle waste of breath to prattle of our achievements, to boast of all that we have done. No refinement of life, no delicacy of taste, no material progress, no sordid heaping up of riches, no sensuous development of art and literature, can in any way compensate for the loss of the great fundamental virtues; and of these great fundamental virtues the greatest is the race's power to perpetuate the race.

Character must show itself in the man's performance both of the duty he owes himself and of the duty he owes the state. The man's foremost duty is owed to himself and his family; and he can do this duty only by earning money, by providing what is essential to material well-being; it is only after this has been done that he can hope to build a higher superstructure on the solid material foundation; it is only after this has been done that he can help in movements for the general well-being. He must pull his own weight first, and only after this can his surplus strength be of use to the general public. It is not good to excite that bitter laughter which expresses contempt; and contempt is what we feel for the being whose enthusiasm to benefit mankind is such that he is a burden to those nearest him; who wishes to do great things for humanity in the abstract, but who can not keep his wife in comfort or educate his children.

Nevertheless, while laying all stress on this point, while not merely acknowledging but insisting upon the fact that there must be a basis of material well-being for the individual as for the nation, let us with equal emphasis insist that this material well-being represents nothing but the foundation, and that the foundation, though indispensable, is worthless unless upon it is raised the superstructure of a higher life. That is why I decline to recognize the mere multimillionaire, the man of mere wealth, as an asset of value to any country; and especially as not an asset to my own country. If he has earned or uses his wealth in a way that makes him of real benefit, of real use—and such is often the case—why, then he does become an asset of worth. But it is the way in which it has been earned or used, and not the mere fact of wealth, that entitles him to the credit. There is need in business, as in most other forms of human activity, of the great guiding intelligences. Their places can not be supplied by any number of lesser intelligences. It is a good thing that they should have ample recognition, ample reward. But we must not transfer our admiration to the reward instead of to the deed rewarded; and if what should be the reward exists without the service having been rendered, then admiration will come only from those who are mean of soul. The truth is that, after a certain measure of tangible material success or reward has been achieved, the question of increasing it becomes of constantly less importance compared to other things that can be done in life. It is a bad thing for a nation to raise and to admire a false standard of success; and there can be no falser standard than that set by the deification of material well-being in and for itself. The man who, for any cause for which he is himself accountable, has failed to support himself and those for whom he is responsible, ought to feel that he has fallen lamentably short in his prime duty. But the man who, having far surpassed the limit of providing for the wants, both of body and mind, of himself and of those depending upon him, then piles up a great fortune, for the acquisition or retention of which he returns no corresponding benefit to the nation as a whole, should himself be made to feel that, so far from being a desirable, he is an unworthy, citizen of the community; that he is to be neither admired nor envied; that his right-thinking fellow countrymen put him low in the scale of citizenship, and leave him to be consoled by the admiration of those whose level of purpose is even lower than his own.

My position as regards the moneyed interests can be put in a few words. In every civilized society property rights must be carefully safeguarded; ordinarily, and in the great majority of cases, human rights and property rights are fundamentally and in the long run identical; but when it clearly appears that there is a real conflict between them, human rights must have the upper hand, for property belongs to man and not man to property.

In fact, it is essential to good citizenship clearly to understand that there are certain qualities which we in a democracy are prone to admire in and of themselves, which ought by rights to be judged admirable or the reverse solely from the standpoint of the use made of them. Foremost among these I should include two very distinct gifts—the gift of money-making and the gift of oratory. Money-making, the money touch, I have spoken of above. It is a quality which in a moderate degree is essential. It may be useful when developed to a very great degree, but only if accompanied and controlled by other qualities; and without such control the possessor tends to develop into one of the least attractive types produced by a modern industrial democracy. So it is with the orator. It is highly desirable that a leader of opinion in a democracy should be able to state his views clearly and convincingly. But all that the oratory can do of value to the community is to enable the man thus to explain himself; if it enables the orator to persuade his hearers to put false values on things, it merely makes him a power for mischief. Some excellent public servants have not the gift at all, and must rely upon their deeds to speak for them; and unless the oratory does represent genuine conviction based on good common sense and able to be translated into efficient performance, then the better the oratory the greater the damage to the public it deceives. Indeed, it is a sign of marked political weakness in any commonwealth if the people tend to be carried away by mere oratory, if they tend to value words in and for themselves, as divorced from the deeds for which they are supposed to stand. The phrase-maker, the phrase-monger, the ready talker, however great his power, whose speech does not make for courage, sobriety, and right understanding, is simply a noxious element in the body politic, and it speaks ill for the public if he has influence over them. To admire the gift of oratory without regard to the moral quality behind the gift is to do wrong to the republic.

Of course all that I say of the orator applies with even greater force to the orator's latter-day and more influential brother, the journalist. The power of the journalist is great, but he is entitled neither to respect nor admiration because of that power unless it is used aright. He can do, and he often does, great good. He can do, and he often does, infinite mischief. All journalists, all writers, for the very reason that they appreciate the vast possibilities of their profession, should bear testimony against those who deeply discredit it. Offences against taste and morals, which are bad enough in a private citizen, are infinitely worse if made into instruments for debauching the community through a newspaper. Mendacity, slander, sensationalism, inanity, vapid triviality, all are potent factors for the debauchery of the public mind and conscience. The excuse advanced for vicious writing, that the public demands it and that the demand must be supplied, can no more be admitted than if it were advanced by the purveyors of food who sell poisonous adulterations.

In short, the good citizen in a republic must realize that he ought to possess two sets of qualities, and that neither avails without the other. He must have those qualities which make for efficiency; and he must also have those qualities which direct the efficiency into channels for the public good. He is useless if he is inefficient. There is nothing to be done with that type of citizen of whom all that can be said is that he is harmless. Virtue which is dependent upon a sluggish circulation is not impressive. There is little place in active life for the timid good man. The man who is saved by weakness from robust wickedness is likewise rendered immune from the robuster virtues. The good citizen in a republic must first of all be able to hold his own. He is no good citizen unless he has the ability which will make him work hard and which at need will make him fight hard. The good citizen is not a good citizen unless he is an efficient citizen.

But if a man's efficiency is not guided and regulated by a moral sense, then the more efficient he is the worse he is, the more dangerous to the body politic. Courage, intellect, all the masterful qualities, serve but to make a man more evil if they are used merely for that man's own advancement, with brutal indifference to the rights of others. It speaks ill for the community if the community worships these qualities and treats their possessors as heroes regardless of whether the qualities are used rightly or wrongly. It makes no difference as to the precise way in which this sinister efficiency is shown. It makes no difference whether such a man's force and ability betray themselves in the career of money-maker or politician, soldier or orator, journalist or popular leader. If the man works for evil, then the more successful he is the more he should be despised and condemned by all upright and far-seeing men. To judge a man merely by success is an abhorrent wrong; and if the people at large habitually so judge men, if they grow to condone wickedness because the wicked man triumphs, they show their inability to understand that in the last analysis free institutions rest upon the character of citizenship, and that by such admiration of evil they prove themselves unfit for liberty.

The homely virtues of the household, the ordinary workaday virtues which make the woman a good housewife and housemother, which make the man a hard worker, a good husband and father, a good soldier at need, stand at the bottom of character. But of course many others must be added thereto if a state is to be not only free but great. Good citizenship is not good citizenship if exhibited only in the home. There remain the duties of the individual in relation to the state, and these duties are none too easy under the conditions which exist where the effort is made to carry on free government in a complex, industrial civilization. Perhaps the most important thing the ordinary citizen, and, above all, the leader of ordinary citizens, has to remember in political life is that he must not be a sheer doctrinaire. The closet philosopher, the refined and cultured individual who from his library tells how men ought to be governed under ideal conditions, is of no use in actual governmental work; and the one-sided fanatic, and still more the mob-leader, and the insincere man who to achieve power promises what by no possibility can be performed, are not merely useless but noxious.

The citizen must have high ideals, and yet he must be able to achieve them in practical fashion. No permanent good comes from aspirations so lofty that they have grown fantastic and have become impossible and indeed undesirable to realize. The impracticable visionary is far less often the guide and precursor than he is the imbittered foe of the real reformer, of the man who, with stumblings and shortcomings, yet does in some shape, in practical fashion, give effect to the hopes and desires of those who strive for better things. Woe to the empty phrase-maker, to the empty idealist, who, instead of making ready the ground for the man of action, turns against him when he appears and hampers him as he does the work! Moreover, the preacher of ideals must remember how sorry and contemptible is the figure which he will cut, how great the damage that he will do, if he does not himself, in his own life, strive measurably to realize the ideals that he preaches for others. Let him remember also that the worth of the ideal must be largely determined by the success with which it can in practice be realized. We should abhor the so-called "practical" men whose practicality assumes the shape of that peculiar baseness which finds its expression in disbelief in morality and decency, in disregard of high standards of living and conduct. Such a creature is the worst enemy of the body politic. But only less desirable as a citizen is his nominal opponent and real ally, the man of fantastic vision who makes the impossible better forever the enemy of the possible good.

We can just as little afford to follow the doctrinaires of an extreme individualism as the doctrinaires of an extreme socialism. Individual initiative, so far from being discouraged, should be stimulated; and yet we should remember that, as society develops and grows more complex, we continually find that things which once it was desirable to leave to individual initiative can, under the changed conditions, be performed with better results by common effort. It is quite impossible, and equally undesirable, to draw in theory a hard-and-fast line which shall always divide the two sets of cases. This every one who is not cursed with the pride of the closet philosopher will see, if he will only take the trouble to think about some of our commonest phenomena. For instance, when people live on isolated farms or in little hamlets, each house can be left to attend to its own drainage and water supply; but the mere multiplication of families in a given area produces new problems which, because they differ in size, are found to differ not only in degree but in kind from the old; and the questions of drainage and water supply have to be considered from the common standpoint. It is not a matter for abstract dogmatizing to decide when this point is reached; it is a matter to be tested by practical experiment. Much of the discussion about socialism and individualism is entirely pointless, because of failure to agree on terminology. It is not good to be the slave of names. I am a strong individualist by personal habit, inheritance, and conviction; but it is a mere matter of common sense to recognize that the state, the community, the citizens acting together, can do a number of things better than if they were left to individual action. The individualism which finds its expression in the abuse of physical force is checked very early in the growth of civilization, and we of to-day should in our turn strive to shackle or destroy that individualism which triumphs by greed and cunning, which exploits the weak by craft instead of ruling them by brutality. We ought to go with any man in the effort to bring about justice and the equality of opportunity, to turn the tool-user more and more into the tool-owner, to shift burdens so that they can be more equitably borne. The deadening effect on any race of the adoption of a logical and extreme socialistic system could not be overstated; it would spell sheer destruction; it would produce grosser wrong and outrage, fouler immorality, than any existing system. But this does not mean that we may not with great advantage adopt certain of the principles professed by some given set of men who happen to call themselves

Socialists; to be afraid to do so would be to make a mark of weakness on our part.

But we should not take part in acting a lie any more than in telling a lie. We should not say that men are equal where they are not equal, nor proceed upon the assumption that there is an equality where it does not exist; but we should strive to bring about a measurable equality, at least to the extent of preventing the inequality which is due to force or fraud. Abraham Lincoln, a man of the plain people, blood of their blood and bone of their bone, who all his life toiled and wrought and suffered for them, and at the end died for them, who always strove to represent them, who would never tell an untruth to or for them, spoke of the doctrine of equality with his usual mixture of idealism and sound common sense. He said (I omit what was of merely local significance):
"I think the authors of the Declaration of Independence intended to include all men, but that they did not mean to declare all men equal *in all respects*. They did not mean to say all men were equal in color, size, intellect, moral development, or social capacity. They defined with tolerable distinctness in what they did consider all men created equal—equal in certain inalienable rights, among which are life, liberty, and the pursuit of happiness. This they said, and this they meant. They did not mean to assert the obvious untruth that all were then actually enjoying that equality, or yet that they were about to confer it immediately upon them. They meant to set up a standard maxim for free society which should be familiar to all—constantly looked to, constantly labored for, and, even though never perfectly attained, constantly approximated, and thereby constantly spreading and deepening its influence, and augmenting the happiness and value of life to all people, everywhere."

We are bound in honor to refuse to listen to those men who would make us desist from the effort to do away with the inequality which means injustice; the inequality of right, of opportunity, of privilege. We are bound in honor to strive to bring ever nearer the day when, as far as is humanly possible, we shall be able to realize the ideal that each man shall have an equal opportunity to show the stuff that is in him by the way in which he renders service. There should, so far as possible, be equality of opportunity to render service; but just so long as there is inequality of service there should and must be inequality of reward. We may be sorry for the general, the painter, the artist, the worker in any profession or of any kind, whose misfortune rather than whose fault it is that he does his work ill. But the reward must go to the man who does his work well; for any other course is to create a new kind of privilege, the privilege of folly and weakness; and special privilege is injustice, whatever form it takes.

To say that the thriftless, the lazy, the vicious, the incapable, ought to have the reward given to those who are far-sighted, capable, and upright, is to say what is not true and can not be true. Let us try to level up, but let us beware of the evil of levelling down. If a man stumbles, it is a good thing to help him to his feet. Every one of us needs a helping hand now and then. But if a man lies down, it is a waste of time to try to carry him; and it is a very bad thing for every one if we make men feel that the same reward will come to those who shirk their work and to those who do it.

Let us, then, take into account the actual facts of life, and not be misled into following any proposal for achieving the millennium, for re-creating the golden age, until we have subjected it to hardheaded examination. On the other hand, it is foolish to reject a proposal merely because it is advanced by visionaries. If a given scheme is proposed, look at it on its merits, and, in considering it, disregard formulas. It does not matter in the least who proposes it, or why. If it seems good, try it. If it proves good, accept it; otherwise reject it. There are plenty of men calling themselves Socialists with whom, up to a certain point, it is quite possible to work. If the next step is one which both we and they wish to take, why of course take it, without any regard to the fact that our views as to the tenth step may differ. But, on the other hand, keep clearly in mind that, though it has been worth while to take one step, this does not in the least mean that it may not be highly disadvantageous to take the next. It is just as foolish to refuse all progress because people demanding it desire at some points to go to absurd extremes, as it would be to go to these absurd extremes simply because some of the measures advocated by the extremists were wise.

The good citizen will demand liberty for himself, and as a matter of pride he will see to it that others receive the liberty which he thus claims as his own. Probably the best test of true love of liberty in any country is the way in which minorities are treated in that country. Not only should there be complete liberty in matters of religion and opinion, but complete liberty for each man to lead his life as he desires, provided only that in so doing he does not wrong his neighbor. Persecution is bad because it is persecution, and without reference to which side happens at the moment to be the persecutor and which the persecuted. Class hatred is bad in just the same way, and without any regard to the individual who, at a given time, substitutes loyalty to a class for loyalty to the nation, or substitutes hatred of men because they happen to come in a certain social category, for judgment awarded them according to their conduct. Remember always that the same measure of condemnation should be extended to the arrogance which would look down upon or crush any man because he is poor and to the envy and hatred which would destroy a man because he is wealthy. The overbearing brutality of the man of wealth or power, and the envious and hateful malice directed against wealth or power, are really at root merely different manifestations of the same quality, merely the two sides of the same shield. The man who, if born to wealth and power, exploits and ruins his less fortunate brethren is at heart the same as the greedy and violent demagogue who excites those who have not property to plunder those who have. The gravest wrong upon his country is inflicted by that man, whatever his station, who seeks to make his countrymen divide primarily on the line that separates class from class, occupation from occupation, men of more wealth from men of less wealth, instead of remembering that the only safe standard is that which judges each man on his worth as a man, whether he be rich or poor, without regard to his profession or to his station in life. Such is the only true democratic test, the only test that can with propriety be applied in a republic. There have been many republics in the past, both in what we call antiquity and in what we call the Middle Ages. They fell, and the prime factor in their fall was the fact that the parties tended to divide along the line that separates wealth from poverty. It made no difference which side was successful; it made no difference whether the republic fell under the rule of an oligarchy or the rule of a mob. In either case, when once loyalty to a class had been substituted for loyalty to the republic, the end of the republic was at hand. There is no greater need to-day than the need to keep ever in mind the fact that the cleavage between right and wrong, between good citizenship and bad citizenship, runs at right angles to, and not parallel with, the lines of cleavage between class and class, between occupation and occupation. Ruin looks us in the face if we judge a man by his position instead of judging him by his conduct in that position.

In a republic, to be successful we must learn to combine intensity of conviction with a broad tolerance of difference of conviction. Wide differences of opinion in matters of religious, political, and social belief must exist if conscience and intellect alike are not to be stunted, if there is to be room for healthy growth. Bitter internecine hatreds, based on such differences, are signs, not of earnestness of belief, but of that fanaticism which, whether religious or anti-religious, democratic or anti-democratic, is itself but a manifestation of the gloomy bigotry which has been the chief factor in the downfall of so many, many nations.

Of one man in especial, beyond any one else, the citizens of a republic should beware, and that is of the man who appeals to them to support him on the ground that he is hostile to other citizens of the republic, that he will secure for those who elect him, in one shape or another, profit at the expense of other citizens of the republic. It makes no difference whether he appeals to class hatred or class interest, to religious or anti-religious prejudice. The man who makes such an appeal should always be presumed to make it for the sake of furthering his own interest. The very last thing that an intelligent and self-respecting member of a democratic community should do is to reward any public man because that public man says he will get the private citizen something to which this private citizen is not entitled, or will gratify some emotion or animosity which this private citizen ought not to possess. Let me illustrate this by one anecdote from my own experience. A number of years ago I was engaged in cattle-ranching on the great plains of the western United States. There were no fences. The cattle wandered free, the ownership of each being determined by the brand; the calves were branded with the brand of the cows they followed. If on the round-up an animal was passed by, the following year it would appear as an unbranded yearling, and was then called a maverick. By the custom of the country these mavericks were branded with the brand of the man on whose range they were found. One day I was riding the range with a newly hired cowboy, and we came upon a maverick. We roped and threw it; then we built a little fire, took out a cinch-ring, heated it at the fire; and the cowboy started to put on the brand. I said to him, "It is So-and-so's brand," naming the man on whose range we happened to be. He answered: "That's all right, boss; I know my business." In another moment I said to him: "Hold on, you are putting on my brand!" To which he answered: "That's all right; I always put on the boss's brand." I answered: "Oh, very well. Now you go straight back to the ranch and get what is owing to you; I don't need you any longer." He jumped up and said: "Why, what's the matter? I was putting on your brand." And I answered: "Yes, my friend, and if you will steal *for* me you will steal *from* me."

Now, the same principle which applies in private life applies also in public life. If a public man tries to get your vote by saying that he will do something wrong *in* your interest, you can be absolutely certain that if ever it becomes worth his while he will do something wrong *against* your interest.

So much for the citizenship of the individual in his relations to his family, to his neighbor, to the state. There remain duties of citizenship which the state, the aggregation of all the individuals, owes in connection with other states, with other nations. Let me say at once that I am no advocate of a foolish cosmopolitanism. I believe that a man must be a good patriot before he can be, and as the only possible way of being, a good citizen of the world. Experience teaches us that the average man who protests that his international feeling swamps his national feeling, that he does not care for his country because he cares so much for mankind, in actual practice proves himself the foe of mankind; that the man who says that he does not care to be a citizen of any one country, because he is a citizen of the world, is in very fact usually an exceedingly undesirable citizen of whatever corner of the world he happens at the moment to be in. In the dim future all moral needs and moral standards may change; but at present, if a man can view his own country and all other countries from the same level with tepid indifference, it is wise to distrust him, just as it is wise to distrust the man who can take the same dispassionate view of his wife and his mother. However broad and deep a man's sympathies, however intense his activities, he need have no fear that they will be cramped by love of his native land.

Now, this does not mean in the least that a man should not wish to do good outside of his native land. On the contrary, just as I think that the man who loves his family is more apt to be a good neighbor than the man who does not, so I think that the most useful member of the family of nations is normally a strongly patriotic nation. So far from patriotism being inconsistent with a proper regard for the rights of other nations, I hold that the true patriot, who is as jealous of the national honor as a gentleman is of his own honor, will be careful to see that the nation neither inflicts nor suffers wrong, just as a gentleman scorns equally to wrong others or to suffer others to wrong him. I do not for one moment admit that political morality is different from private morality, that a promise made on the stump differs from a promise made in private life. I do not for one moment admit that a man should act deceitfully as a public servant in his dealings with other nations, any more than that he should act deceitfully in his dealings as a private citizen with other private citizens. I do not for one moment admit that a nation should treat other nations in a different spirit from that in which an honorable man would treat other men.

In practically applying this principle to the two sets of cases there is, of course, a great practical difference to be taken into account. We speak of international law; but international law is something wholly different from private or municipal law, and the capital difference is that there is a sanction for the one and no sanction for the other; that there is an outside force which compels individuals to obey the one, while there is no such outside force to compel obedience as regards the other. International law will, I believe, as the generations pass, grow stronger and stronger until in some way or other there develops the power to make it respected. But as yet it is only in the first formative period. As yet, as a rule, each nation is of necessity obliged to judge for itself in matters of vital importance between it and its neighbors, and actions must of necessity, where this is the case, be different from what they are where, as among private citizens, there is an outside force whose action is all-powerful and must be invoked in any crisis of importance. It is the duty of wise statesmen, gifted with the power of looking ahead, to try to encourage and build up every movement which will substitute or tend to substitute some other agency for force in the settlement of international disputes. It is the duty of every honest statesman to try to guide the nation so that it shall not wrong any other nation. But as yet the great civilized peoples, if they are to be true to themselves and to the cause of humanity and civilization, must keep ever in mind that in the last resort they must possess both the will and the power to resent wrong-doing from others. The men who sanely believe in a lofty morality preach righteousness; but they do not preach weakness, whether among private citizens or among nations. We believe that our ideals should be high, but not so high as to make it impossible measurably to realize them. We sincerely and earnestly believe in peace; but if peace and justice conflict, we scorn the man who would not stand for justice though the whole world came in arms against him.

And now, my hosts, a word in parting. You and I belong to the only two republics among the great powers of the world. The ancient friendship between France and the United States has been, on the whole, a sincere and disinterested friendship. A calamity to you would be a sorrow to us. But it would be more than that. In the seething turmoil of the history of humanity certain nations stand out as possessing a peculiar power or charm, some special gift of beauty or wisdom or strength, which puts them among the immortals, which makes them rank forever with the leaders of mankind. France is one of these nations. For her to sink would be a loss to all the world. There are certain lessons of brilliance and of generous gallantry that she can teach better than any of her sister nations. When the French peasantry sang of Malbrook, it was to tell how the soul of this warrior-foe took flight upward through the laurels he had won. Nearly seven centuries ago, Froissart, writing of a time of dire disaster, said that the realm of France was never so stricken that there were not left men who would valiantly fight for it. You have had a great past. I believe that you will have a great future. Long may you carry yourselves proudly as citizens of a nation which bears a leading part in the teaching and uplifting of mankind.

The Leader and The Cause
"It Takes More Than That
to Kill a Bull Moose"

On October 14, 1912, before Roosevelt entered an auditorium in Milwaukee, Wisconsin to make a speech, he was shot in an assassination attempt. The full account of the incident including the description "Col. Roosevelt delivered part of his scheduled address with the bullet in his body, his blood staining his white vest as he spoke to a huge throng at the auditorium" follows the text of this speech.

Friends, I shall ask you to be as quiet as possible. I don't know whether you fully understand that I have just been shot; but it takes more than that to kill a Bull Moose. But fortunately I had my manuscript, so you see I was going to make a long speech, and there is a bullet—there is where the bullet went through— and it probably saved me from it going into my heart. The bullet is in me now, so that I cannot make a very long speech, but I will try my best.

And now, friends, I want to take advantage of this incident to say a word of solemn warning to my fellow countrymen. First of all, I want to say this about myself: I have altogether too important things to think of to feel any concern over my own death; and now I cannot speak to you insincerely within five minutes of being shot. I am telling you the literal truth when I say that my concern is for many other things. It is not in the least for my own life. I want you to understand that I am ahead of the game, anyway. No man has had a happier life than I have led; a happier life in every way. I have been able to do certain things that I greatly wished to do, and I am interested in doing other things. I can tell you with absolute truthfulness that I am very much uninterested in whether I am shot or not. It was just as when I was colonel of my regiment. I always felt that a private was to be excused for feeling at times some pangs of anxiety about his personal safety, but I cannot understand a man fit to be a colonel who can pay any heed to his personal safety when he is occupied as he ought to be with the absorbing desire to do his duty.

I am in this cause with my whole heart and soul. I believe that the Progressive movement is making life a little easier for all our people; a movement to try to take the burdens off the men and especially the women and children of this country. I am absorbed in the success of that movement.

Friends, I ask you now this evening to accept what I am saying as absolutely true, when I tell you I am not thinking of my own success. I am not thinking of my life or of anything connected with me personally. I am thinking of the movement. I say this by way of introduction, because I want to say something very serious to our people and especially to the newspapers. I don't know anything about who the man was who shot me to-night. He was seized at once by one of the stenographers in my party, Mr. Martin, and I suppose is now in the hands of the police. He shot to kill. He shot—the shot, the bullet went in here —I will show you.

I am going to ask you to be as quiet as possible for I am not able to give to challenge of the bull moose quite as loudly.

Now, I do not know who he was or what he represented. He was a coward. He stood in the darkness in the crowd around the automobile and when they cheered me, and I got up to bow, he stepped forward and shot me in the darkness.

Now, friends, of course, I do not know, as I say, anything about him; but it is a very natural thing that weak and vicious minds should be inflamed to acts of violence by the kind of awful mendacity and abuse that have been heaped upon me for the last three months by the papers in the interest of not only Mr. Debs but of Mr. Wilson and Mr. Taft.

Friends, I will disown and repudiate any man of my party who attacks with such foul slander and abuse any opponent of any other party; and now I wish to say seriously to all the daily newspapers, to the Republicans, the Democrat, and Socialist parties, that they cannot, month in month out and year in and year out, make the kind of untruthful, of bitter assault that they have made and not expect that brutal, violent natures, or brutal and violent characters, especially when the brutality is accompanied by a not very strong mind; they cannot expect that such natures will be unaffected by it.

Now, friends, I am not speaking for myself at all, I give you my word, I do not care a rap about being shot; not a rap.

I have had a good many experiences in my time and this is one of them. What I care for is my country. I wish I were able to impress upon my people—our people, the duty to feel strongly but to speak the truth of their opponents. I say now, I have never said one word on the stump against any opponent that I cannot defend. I have said nothing that I could not substantiate and nothing that I ought not to have said— nothing that I—nothing that, looking back at, I would not say again.

Now, friends, it ought not to be too much to ask that our opponents — *[speaking to somebody on the stage who was apparently trying to get him to finish the speech and get medical attention]* — I am not sick at all. I am all right. I cannot tell you of what infinitesimal importance I regard this incident as compared with the great issues at stake in this campaign, and I ask it not for my sake, not the least in the world, but for the sake of common country, that they make up their minds to speak only the truth, and not use that kind of slander and mendacity which if taken seriously must incite weak and violent natures to crimes of violence. Don't you make any mistake. Don't you pity me. I am all right. I am all right and you cannot escape listening to the speech either.

And now, friends, this incident that has just occurred—this effort to assassinate me—emphasizes to a peculiar degree the need of the Progressive movement. Friends, every good citizen ought to do everything in his or her power to prevent the coming of the day when we shall see in this country two recognized creeds fighting one another, when we shall see the creed of the "Havenots" arraigned against the creed of the "Haves." When that day comes then such incidents as this to-night will be commonplace in our history. When you make poor men—when you permit the conditions to grow such that the poor man as such will be swayed by his sense of injury against the men who try to hold what they improperly have won, when that day comes, the most awful passions will be let loose and it will be an ill day for our country.

Now, friends, what we who are in this movement are endeavoring to do is forestall any such movement for justice now—a movement in which we ask all just men of generous hearts to join with the men who feel in their souls that lift upward which bids them refuse to be satisfied themselves while their countrymen and countrywomen suffer from avoidable misery. Now, friends, what we Progressives are trying to do is to enroll rich or poor, whatever their social or industrial position, to stand together for the most elementary rights of good citizenship, those elementary rights which are the foundation of good citizenship in this great Republic of ours.

[At this point a renewed effort was made to persuade Roosevelt to finish the speech and get medical attention]

My friends are a little more nervous than I am. Don't you waste any sympathy on me. I have had an A-1 time in life and I am having it now.

I never in my life was in any movement in which I was able to serve with such whole-hearted devotion as in this; in which I was able to feel as I do in this that common weal. I have fought for the good of our common country.

And now, friends, I shall have to cut short much of that speech that I meant to give you, but I want to touch on just two or three points.

In the first place, speaking to you here in Milwaukee, I wish to say that the Progressive party is making its appeals to all our fellow citizens without any regard to their creed or to their birthplace. We do not regard as essential the way in which a man worships his God or as being affected by where he was born. We regard it as a matter of spirit and purpose. In New York, while I was police commissioner, the two men from whom I got the most assistance were Jacob Riis, who was born in Denmark, and Arthur von Briesen, who was born in Germany—both of them as fine examples of the best and highest American citizenship as you could find in any part of this country.

I have just been introduced by one of your own men here—Henry Cochems. His grandfather, his father, and that father's seven brothers, all served in the United States army, and they entered it four years after they had come to this country from Germany. Two of them left their lives, spent their lives, on the field of battle. I am all right—I am a little sore. Anybody has a right to be sore with a bullet in him. You would find that if I was in battle now I would be leading my men just the same. Just the same way I am going to make this speech.

At one time I promoted five men for gallantry on the field of battle. Afterward in making some inquiries about them I found that two of them were Protestants, two Catholic, and one a Jew. One Protestant came from Germany and one was born in Ireland. I did not promote them because of their religion. It just happened that way. If all five of them had been Jews I would have promoted them, or if all five of them had been Protestants I would have promoted them; or if they had been Catholics. In that regiment I had a man born in Italy who distinguished himself by gallantry; there was another young fellow, a son of Polish parents, and another who came here when he was a child from Bohemia, who likewise distinguished themselves; and friends, I assure you, that I was incapable of considering any question whatever, but the worth of each individual as a fighting man. If he was a good fighting man, then I saw that Uncle Sam got the benefit of it. That is all.

I make the same appeal to our citizenship. I ask in our civic life that we in the same way pay heed only to the man's quality of citizenship, to repudiate as the worst enemy that we can have whoever tries to get us to discriminate for or against any man because of his creed or birthplace.

Now, friends, in the same way I want out people to stand by one another without regard to differences or class or occupation. I have always stood by labor-unions. I am going to make one omission to-night. I have prepared my speech because Mr. Wilson had seen fit to attack me by showing up his record in comparison with mine. But I am not going to do that to-night. I am going to simply speak of what I myself have done and what I think ought to be done in this country of ours.

It is essential that here should be organizations of labor. This is an era of organization. Capital organizes and therefore labor must organize. My appeal for organized labor is two-fold; to the outsider and the capitalist I make my appeal to treat the laborer fairly, to recognize the fact that he must organize that there must be such organization, that the laboring man must organize for his own protection, and that it is the duty of the rest of is to help him and not hinder him in organizing. That is one-half appeal that I make.

Now, the other half is to the labor man himself. My appeal to him is to remember that as he wants justice, so he must do justice. I want every labor man, every labor leader, every organized union man, to take the lead in denouncing disorder and in denouncing the inciting of riot; that in this country we shall proceed under the protection of our laws and with all respect to the laws, I want the labor men to feel in their turn that exactly as justice must be done them so they must do justice. They must bear their duty as citizens, their duty to this great country of ours, and that they must not rest content unless they do that duty to the fullest degree.

[I know these doctors, when they get hold of me, will never let me go back, and there are just a few more things that I want to say to you.]

And here I have got to make one comparison between Mr. Wilson and myself, simply because he has invited it and I cannot shrink from it. Mr. Wilson has seen fit to attack me, to say that I did not do much against the trusts when I was President. I have got two answers to make to that. In the first place what I did, and then I want to compare what I did when I was President with what Mr. Wilson did not do when he was governor.

When I took the office the antitrust law was practically a dead letter and the interstate commerce law in as poor a condition. I had to revive both laws. I did. I enforced both. It will be easy enough to do now what I did then, but the reason that it is easy now is because I did it when it was hard.

Nobody was doing anything. I found speedily that the interstate commerce law by being made perfect could be made a most useful instrument for helping solve some of our industrial problems. So with the antitrust law. I speedily found out that almost the only positive good achieved by such a successful lawsuit as the Northern Securities suit, for instance, was in establishing the principle that the government was supreme over the big corporation, but by itself that the law did not accomplish any of the things that we ought to have accomplished; and so I began to fight for the amendment of the law along the lines of the interstate commerce law, and now we propose, we Progressives, to establish and interstate commission having the same power over industrial concerns that the Interstate Commerce Commission has over railroads, so that whenever there is in the future a decision rendered in such important matters as the recent suits against the Standard Oil, the Sugar—no, not that—Tobacco—Tobacco Trust—we will have a commission which will see that the decree of the court is really made effective; that it is not made a merely nominal decree.

Our opponents have said that we intend to legalize monopoly. Nonsense. They have legalized monopoly. At this moment the Standard Oil and Tobacco Trust monopolies are legalized; they are being carried on under the decree of the Supreme Court. Our proposal is really to break up monopoly. Our proposal is to lay down certain requirements, and then to require the commerce commission—the industrial commission—to see that the trusts live up to those requirements. Our opponents have spoken as if we were going to let the commission declare what those requirements should be. Not at all. We are going to put the requirements in the law and then see that the commission requires them to obey that law.

And now, friends, as Mr. Wilson has invited the comparison, I only want to say this: Mr. Wilson has said that the States are the proper authorities to deal with the trusts. Well, about eighty percent of the trusts are organized in New Jersey. The Standard Oil, the Tobacco, the Sugar, the Beef, all those trusts are organized in the state of New Jersey and the laws of New Jersey say that their charters can at any time be amended or repealed if they misbehave themselves and give the government ample power to act about those laws, and Mr. Wilson has been governor a year and nine months and he has not opened his lips. The chapter describing what Mr. Wilson has done about trusts in New Jersey would read precisely like a chapter describing snakes in Ireland, which ran: "There are no snakes in Ireland." Mr. Wilson has done precisely and exactly nothing about the trusts.

I tell you, and I told you at the beginning, I do not say anything on the stump that I do not believe. I do not say anything I do not know. Let any of Mr. Wilson's friends on Tuesday point out one thing or let Mr. Wilson point out one thing that he has done about the trusts as governor of New Jersey.

And now, friends, there is one thing I want to say especially to you people here in Wisconsin. All that I have said so far is what I would say in any part of the Union. I have a peculiar right to ask that in this great contest you men and women of Wisconsin shall stand with us. You have taken the lead in progressive movements here in Wisconsin. You have taught the rest of us to look to you for inspiration and leadership. Now, friends, you have made that movement here locally. You will being doing a dreadful injustice to yourselves; you will be doing a dreadful injustice to the rest of us throughout the Union, if you fail to stand with us now that we are making this national movement. What I am about to say now I want you to understand. If I speak of Mr. Wilson I speak with no mind of bitterness. I merely want to discuss the difference of policy between the Progressive and the Democratic party and to ask you to think for yourselves which party you will follow. I will say that, friends, because the Republican party is beaten. Nobody needs to have any idea that anything can be done with the Republican party.

When the Republican party—not the Republican party—when the bosses in control of the Republican party, the Barneses and Penroses, last June stole the nomination and wrecked the Republican party for good and all—I want to point out to you that nominally they stole that nomination from me, but it was really from you. They did not like me, and the longer they live the less cause they will have to like me. But while they don't like me, they dread you. You are the people that they dread. They dread the people themselves, and those bosses and the big special interests behind them made up their mind that they would rather see the Republican party wrecked than see it come under the control of the people themselves. So I am not dealing with the Republican party. There are only two ways you can vote this year. You can be progressive or reactionary. Whether you vote Republican or Democratic it does not make a difference, you are voting reactionary.

Now, the Democratic Party in its platform and through the utterances of Mr. Wilson has distinctly committed itself to the old flintlock, muzzle-loaded doctrine of States' rights, and I have said distinctly we are for people's rights. We are for the rights of the people. If they can be obtained best through National Government, then we are for national rights. We are for people's rights however it is necessary to secure them.

Mr. Wilson has made a long essay against Senator Beveridge's bill to abolish child labor. It is the same kind of argument that would be made against our bill to prohibit women from working more than eight hours a day in industry. It is the same kind of argument that would have to be made; if it is true, it would apply equally against our proposal to insist that in continuous industries there shall be by law one day's rest in seven and three-shift eight-hour day. You have labor laws here in Wisconsin, and chamber of commerce will tell you that because of that fact there are industries that will not come to Wisconsin. They prefer to stay outside where they can work children of tender years, where they can work women fourteen and sixteen hours a day, where if it is a continuous industry, they can work men twelve hours a day and seven days a week.

Now, friends, I know that you of Wisconsin would never repeal those laws even if they are at your commercial hurt, just as I am trying to get New York to adopt such laws even though it will be to the New York's commercial hurt. But if possible I want to arrange it so that we can have justice without commercial hurt, and you can only get that if you have justice enforced nationally. You won't be burdened in Wisconsin with industries not coming to the State if the same good laws are extended all over the other States. Do you see what I mean? The States all compete in a common market; and it is not justice to the employers of a State that has enforced just and proper laws to have them exposed to the competition of another State where no such laws are enforced. Now, the Democratic platform, and their speakers declare we shall not have such laws. Mr. Wilson has distinctly declared that we shall not have a national law to prohibit the labor of children, to prohibit child labor. He has distinctly declared that we shall not have a law to establish a minimum wage for women.

I ask you to look at our declaration and hear and read our platform about social and industrial justice and then, friends, vote for the Progressive ticket without regard to me, without regard to my personality, for only by voting for that platform can you be true to the cause of progress throughout this Union.

October 15, 1912 *Detroit Free Press* Front Page Story about the Assassination Attempt on Roosevelt Prior to His Speech

Milwaukee, Wis., October 14 -- A desperate attempt to kill Col. Theodore Roosevelt tonight failed when a 32 caliber bullet aimed directly at the heart of the former president and fired at short range by the crazed assailant, spent part of its force in a bundle of manuscript containing the address which Col. Roosevelt was to deliver tonight, and wounded the Progressive candidate for President.

Col. Roosevelt delivered part of his scheduled address with the bullet in his body, his blood staining his white vest as he spoke to a huge throng at the auditorium. Later, he collapsed, weakened by the wound, and was rushed to Emergency hospital.

Shot in Front of Hotel
The shooting took place in the street in front of the Hotel Gilpatrick. Col. Roosevelt reached Milwaukee shortly after 5 o'clock and making his way through the crowd which had gathered at the station, entered an automobile and was driven to a private dining room on the main floor with the members of the party on his private car.

After dinner Col. Roosevelt stood up, waving his hat in answer to the cheers of the crowd. The assassin was standing in the crowd a few feet from the automobile. He pushed his way to the side of the car and, raising his gun, fired.

Henry F. Cochems, former athlete and Chairman of the Progressive Party speaker's bureau, and Elbert Martin, Roosevelt's stenographer, seized the man and held him until policemen came up. John Schrank, who is small of stature, admitted firing the shot and said that "any man looking for a third term ought to be shot."

Col. Roosevelt barely moved as the shot was fired. Before the crowd knew what had happened, Martin, who is six feet tall and a former football player, had landed squarely on the assassin's shoulders and borne him to the ground. He threw his right arm about the man's neck with a death-like grip and with his left arm seized the hand that held the revolver. In another second he had disarmed him.

All this happened within a few seconds and Col. Roosevelt stood gazing rather curiously at the man who attempted his life before the stunned crowd realized what was going on. Col. Roosevelt refused to allow doctors to examine him at first. Later, doctors made an examination of the wound and announced "Col. Roosevelt is suffering from a superficial flesh wound. Bleeding was insignificant. He soon traveled on to the Auditorium where he was scheduled to give a speech."

Bullet Perforates Manuscript
The manuscript of his speech doubtless had done much to save his life. When he had come upon the platform at the Auditorium he drew the manuscript from his vest pocket during his first few words, the torn sheets of paper, showing many stains blood, showed also that the bullet had gone through the manuscript. "You see," cried the colonel holding up the manuscript so that the audience could see the bullet hole through the sheets of paper, "It takes more than that to kill a Bull Moose."

Teddy Roosevelt Saves Football

American football is incredibly popular, but did you know that if it wasn't for Teddy Roosevelt, the sport might not be played at all -- or at least played as we know and love it today?

Following the 2010 season, Harris Interactive's annual survey shows that professional football (NFL) is the most popular sport in America followed by professional baseball (MLB) and college football. Overall 31% of American adults said the NFL was their favorite sport followed by the MLB with 17% and college football with 12%.

In 2010, the NFL TV ratings showed the average regular season audience at 17.9 million viewers. The 4 games on the first weekend of the playoffs averaged 32.3 million viewers. And, for the second year in a row, the Super Bowl set a record for American television viewing with an estimated 111 million people watching the Green Bay Packers defeat the Pittsburgh Steelers (according to The Nielsen Co.)

According to the National Football Foundation & College Hall of Fame, in the 2010 season:

- The 120 schools from the NCAA Football Bowl Subdivision drew a record 37,678,722 fans.
- 13 shools -- Alabama, Auburn, Florida, Georgia, LSU, Michigan, Nebraska, Ohio State, Oklahoma, Penn State, Tennessee, Texas and South Carolina -- played in front of more than one million fans during the 2010 season.

- Approximately 200 million tuned in to watch college football regular-season games on ESPN, ESPN2 and ABC.
- The 35 post-season bowl games drew an all-time high of 1,813,215 spectators for an average of 51,806.

Yep, we Americans love our football ... but, why give Teddy Roosevelt credit for the sport and our passion for it?

In the early 1900's, the game of football was played primarily on college campuses and it was incredibly rough with typical game conduct including gang tackling, punching and unsportsmanlike behavior. Many young men were actually killed during games. In fact, with about 20 times fewer players than there are today, 18 players died in 1905 alone.

Not surprisingly, a prohibition movement was started to ban the sport (led by Charles Eliot the president of Harvard). But Roosevelt liked the game. He felt it built strong bodies, character, a sense of team and an attitude of never giving up. In fact, 10 of the Rough Riders (the soldiers who fought with TR in Cuba) gave their occupations as football players when they enlisted in 1898.

So in 1905, Roosevelt gathered representatives of the "Big 3" (Harvard, Yale and Princeton, the universities who first played the game and who also set the rules of play) at to the White House and convinced them to keep football but to change the rules to eliminate the foul play and brutality.

As a result of that meeting, the American Football Rules Committee was formed and, in 1906, plays designed to open up the game and make it less dangerous to play were introduced, including:

- the distance to be gained for a first down was increased from five to ten yards
- all mass formations and gang tackling was banned
- the forward pass was introduced
- a neutral zone at the line of scrimmage was established

As a result of those rule changes, football became less dangerous to play – injuries and deaths decreased – and it became more fun to watch.

Teddy Roosevelt had saved football!

And, as one of the 111 million people who watched the Super Bowl XLV, "Thanks, TR!"

> NOTE: At the time of this writing, with the epidemic of head, neck and spinal injuries, and the blurring of lines between college and pro ballplayers, American football is facing challenging times. Perhaps, just as Teddy Roosevelt did last century, a leader who can bring together the forces of contemporary football will step forward to generate positive change that will move the game forward for the next 100 years.

THE "WORDS & WISDOM" SERIES

Available from Amazon.com and other retailers

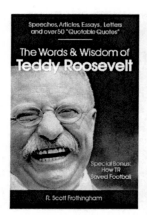

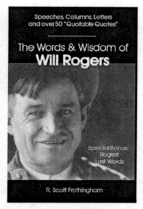

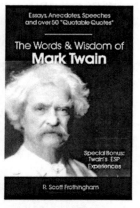

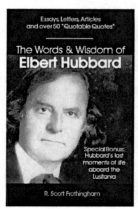

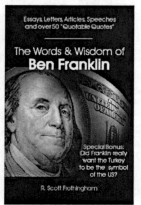

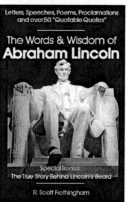

Selections of the actual words of historical figures
that will give you a better understanding of
the people behind the beloved icons and notable events.

ABOUT THE AUTHOR

Scott Frothingham is an entrepreneur, consultant, speaker, business coach and author best known for his FastForward Income™ products including *The 15-minute Sales Workout*™. He helps entrepreneurs, managers and sales/marketing executives position themselves for success through skills training and personal development -- along with providing tools for effectively and efficiently training and motivating their teams.

R. Scott Frothingham

www.ScottFrothingham.com

Facebook: **www.Facebook.com/FastForwardIncome**

Twitter: **@ScottFroth**

www.FastForwardPublishing.com

Edward S. Ellis is best known for his youth-targeted fictional works in the American dime, pulp, and series novel genre like *Seth Jones* or *The Captives of the Frontier* (described as the "perfect dime novel" of thrilling frontier adventure -- estimated 60,000 copies in its first week and 450,000 copies in its first six months), *The Huge Hunter* or *The Steam Man of the Prairies* (first U.S. science fiction dime novel) and the series featuring Native American: Deerfoot. Later in life he turned to more serious work, writing accounts of historical events and biographies, mostly for adults.

For more details on the life, career and books of Edward S. Ellis, visit **www.EdwardSEllis.com**.

www.FastForwardPublishing.com

CPSIA information can be obtained at www.ICGtesting.com
Printed in the USA
LVOW08s0249091014

407987LV00008B/104/P